Avoiding the Trap
of Being Offended

Avoiding the Trap
of Being Offended

by
Kenneth W. Hagin

14 13 12 11 10 09 08   07 06 05 04 03 02 01

Avoiding the Trap of Being Offended

In the U.S. write:
Kenneth Hagin Ministries
P.O. Box 50126
Tulsa, OK 74150-0126
1-888-28-FAITH
www.rhema.org

In Canada write:
Kenneth Hagin Ministries
P.O. Box 335, Station D
Etobicoke (Toronto), Ontario
Canada, M9A 4X3
1-866-70-RHEMA
www.rhemacanada.org

Contents

Preface

Many good books have been written about faith and about how to receive from God. Most of us understand the principles at work when Jesus cursed the fig tree and saw the fruit of His spoken words. After the disciples took notice of the withered tree, Jesus explained to them, "Have the faith of God" (Mark 11:22), or have the God-kind of faith.

We as believers are supposed to have the God-kind of faith, and we're supposed to use our faith effectively. But having productive faith is not possible without operating in the God-kind of *love*. In other words, the verses we love and shout about are indeed true, but so are the verses that are more sobering. *All* of Scripture is infallible, immutable, and true!

So before we speak to the mountains in our lives and command them to be removed (Mark 11:23), we need to get hold of another equally powerful truth found in Mark 11:25–26. We must begin plucking up roots of bitterness and unforgiveness that have held us back from succeeding as we should. As Christians, we are supposed to forgive others just as God has forgiven us.

Many people remember my father as a great man of faith. And it's true—Dad did have a revelation of faith in God's Word that changed his life and the lives of countless others too. But Kenneth E. Hagin was better known as being a great man of *love*. And not only did my father live a life of love and forgiveness, he taught others to do the same. Anyone who knew him knew that he never held a grudge against anyone, and he never said anything bad about anyone. Dad's faith worked, and he could walk by faith so proficiently, because he also walked *in love*.

At my father's memorial service, many spoke about their memories of him, and over and over we heard people saying the same thing—that Dad always forgave and kept a good report no matter what. My father had that testimony because he understood the powerful truths of love and forgiveness. In his lifetime, he taught prosperity, and he walked in prosperity. He taught healing, and he walked in healing. But my dad didn't just love the messages of prosperity and healing. He loved *the whole counsel of God's Word*.

As a minister of the Gospel myself, I am interested in people having their needs met, growing in grace, and becoming fruitful in the Kingdom of God through their knowledge of the Word. I see so many confused Christians whose faith has been all but shipwrecked because they thought they were standing their ground in faith, yet something bad happened. I can't pretend to know all the answers as to why people fail to receive from God. But I can present one very good reason in the pages of this book, and that is the subtle tool of the enemy called *offense*.

As believers, every one of us can receive from God and walk in His highest and best. But we must avoid this trap called offense by recognizing and avoiding this deadly deception of the enemy. I encourage you to make this a priority in your life. My prayer is that this book will guide you and help you learn to succeed in avoiding the trap of being offended.

Kenneth W. Hagin

Chapter 1

Why Fail When You Can Forgive?

Returning on foot from Bethany to Jerusalem that ordinary spring morning, Jesus noticed a fig tree, its sprawling branches conspicuously adorned with leaves. Approaching the tree, He paused to look for a few early figs. Obviously disappointed by the tree's barrenness, Jesus spoke with commanding authority, *"Let no fruit grow on you ever again"* (See Matt. 21:19 NKJV; Mark 11:14).

Later, when the disciples noticed the tree's lifeless, withered branches, they couldn't help but be amazed by its subservience to the Master. Jesus had attempted to glean fruit from this tree, a commonplace act in that day and time. But this ordinary event was transformed into something remarkable and extraordinary in the hearts and minds of Jesus' followers.

What had just occurred? A better question might be *how had this occurred?* Jesus, the Son of God, led by the Holy Spirit in thought, word, and action, had exhibited a higher order of any faith or power than the disciples had ever known.

Through example, Jesus was showing them *and us* how to walk, live, serve, and minister in His absence: *by the faith of God.*

MARK 11:21–24

21 And Peter calling to remembrance saith unto him, Master, behold, the fig tree which thou cursedst is withered away.

22 And Jesus answering saith unto them, Have faith in God.

23 For verily I say unto you, That whosoever shall say unto this mountain, Be thou removed, and be thou cast into the sea; and shall not doubt in his heart, but shall believe that those things which he saith shall come to pass; he shall have whatsoever he saith.

24 Therefore I say unto you, What things soever ye desire, when ye pray, believe that ye receive them, and ye shall have them.

Many Christians become thrilled when they read these verses of Scripture. I do too! It's the Word of God, and God's Word *should* invigorate and energize the believer. The Word of God should create within him or her a solid faith and the confident expectation that what God promised, He is faithful to do! Jesus carried that expectation and taught us to do the same when He said, *". . . Have faith in God"* (v. 22).

However, as a minister of the Gospel who will one day answer to Christ for the way I fulfilled my ministry, I cannot preach or teach just the parts of the Bible that make people excited enough to want to jump, dance, or yell, "Hallelujah!" I must be careful to minister the *whole* counsel of God. That means teaching the "exciting" parts and the parts that don't seem nearly as exciting.

For example, God is just as faithful to perfect that which concerns you and me (Ps. 138:8; Phil. 1:6) as He is to fulfill all of his promises. He is just as faithful to deal with us about some area of our lives that isn't lining up with His Word as He is to honor the Word we're standing on to receive something from Him.

Some people don't want to hear about the "perfecting" or maturing parts of the Scripture, yet those parts help make up the whole counsel of God, the Bible, nonetheless.

In fact, if people won't hear the *correction* of the Bible, they will not likely receive and enjoy the *blessings* of the Bible.

Why We Need a Balanced Message in Order to Succeed

I believe we're living in a day the Apostle Paul warned us about in Second Timothy 4:3.

2 TIMOTHY 4:3 (NIV)

3 For the time will come when men will not put up with sound doctrine. Instead, to suit their own desires, they will gather around them a great number of teachers to say what their itching ears want to hear.

There are more doctrinal truths in the Word of God than just the messages of faith and prosperity. But you almost wouldn't know it by the way some Christians act. Some believers will actually walk out of a service if the minister isn't preaching or teaching on the subject of faith and how to receive from God. It's as if they won't endure or put up with any other sound doctrine. What they don't realize is that *all* truth from the Bible is needed to maintain a stable, steady Christian walk and to become the full-grown man or woman of God that He intends.

Some people just don't want to hear that kind of preaching and teaching, because they want to live the way *they* want to live and then try to make the Word of God support their lifestyle. Any one of us could slip into that subtle way of thinking. That's why our constant attitude should be, *It's not what I want, but what GOD wants that matters. And it's not what I say or what anyone else says—it's what HE says that counts!*

Certainly, I believe in faith and prosperity. I know that God desires to bless us. In fact, He *delights* in our prosperity, and it is His *pleasure* to give us the kingdom (Ps. 35:27; Luke 12:32). But I also believe that we need to look at the *whole* counsel of God's Word and not just the bits and pieces that we especially like.

When I was in elementary school, we were taught a class about health and nutrition. Our teacher stressed the importance of eating a balanced diet and taught us what back then was considered the Seven Basic Food Groups. She told us that foods from each of these groups worked together to nourish us and keep us healthy. She was talking about eating a *balanced* diet.

To illustrate the effects of eating a balanced diet, the teacher showed us a picture of a big, strong man, whom she pointed out always ate his green vegetables and carrots along with his meat and potatoes!

I don't know too many children who will automatically choose green vegetables, such as spinach, over other foods, such as potatoes, corn, bread, or milk. That's why kids have to be *taught* how to keep their bodies nourished properly.

Then to illustrate the effects of a *lack* of balance in diet, our teacher showed the class a picture of a skinny, scrawny man who looked weak and emaciated. This guy had eaten only foods he liked, especially sweets.

What message was our teacher trying to get across to us? She wasn't telling us never to eat candy or sweets. She was telling us that eating too many foods from one food group while not eating enough from other food groups would affect our physical health and well-being.

The same is true spiritually. If we focus only on one or two subjects from the Word of God and neglect to receive from other areas of the Word, we will become weak and unproductive spiritually.

I enjoy hearing a good message on prosperity. But if that's all I ever listened to, I would become lopsided in my spiritual walk. There's nothing wrong with preaching or teaching about divine prosperity, but the message won't work or produce fruit in our lives if we're refusing to hear the whole counsel of God.

Faith and Forgiveness

Can you then see why confessing the Word over your circumstances won't produce anything if you're holding unforgiveness in your heart against someone? If you understand the principles of *faith,* but you don't understand principles of *forgiveness,* you're going to be weak and unstable in your Christian walk. You won't be the best you can be like the strong man in those pictures I saw as a young schoolboy.

My father, Kenneth E. Hagin, lived a life of faith, but he also lived a life free of offense. If you knew anything about Dad at all, you'd know that he never said anything bad about anyone no matter what. He gained the reputation for being strong in faith because he also walked in love.

When someone fails to receive something from God that He has promised in His Word, the problem is never with God. My dad used to say, "We need to find out how God works and work with Him, not against Him." It's true. When we experience failure in life, we need to be honest enough to admit that we missed it somewhere, because God never fails. He never misses it, but we *can* miss it.

Don't misunderstand me. Some Christians become so focused on where they may have missed it that their faith is rendered useless. We can ask God to show us if we've missed it somewhere, and He *will* show us. We don't have to go looking for "hidden" sin in our lives or allow condemnation to beat us up and rob us of faith and the blessings of God. We can know in our heart when we've done something wrong.

One example of something from the Word that can cause a person's faith to fail is unforgiveness, or *offense*. Becoming offended and holding a grudge in your heart will keep your faith from being effective or fruitful.

It's been said that harboring offense is like drinking poison and expecting someone else to die from it! What is offense? Some of the words for "offend" in its various forms ("offense"; "take offense") are as follows:

- *to entrap or impede*

- *to make to stumble and fall or to entice to sin*

- *to cause one to judge another unfavorably or unjustly*

- *to cause or to create displeasure, resentment, or anger*

- *to give offense; to hurt; to insult*

- *to take hurt*

- *to fall into misery; to become wretched*

See the Whole Picture

We already read Mark 11:22–24: *". . . Have faith in God. For verily I say unto you, That whosoever shall say unto this mountain, Be thou removed, and be thou cast into the sea; and shall not doubt in his heart, but shall believe that those things which he saith shall come to pass; he shall have whatsoever he saith. Therefore I say unto you, What things soever ye desire, when ye pray, believe that ye receive them, and ye shall have them."*

The discourse that Jesus began in verse 22 doesn't end with verse 24. However, that's where many people stop when talking about faith. Yet there are two more verses after verse 24 that complete the picture—the context of Jesus' teaching.

MARK 11:25–26

25 And when ye stand [or sit or kneel] praying, FOR-GIVE, if ye have ought against any: that your Father also which is in heaven may forgive you your trespasses.

26 But if ye DO NOT FORGIVE, neither will your Father which is in heaven forgive your trespasses.

Let's look at those verses in *The Amplified Bible.*

MARK 11:25–26 (Amplified)

25 And whenever you stand praying, if you have anything against anyone, forgive him and let it drop [leave it, let it go], in order that your Father Who is in heaven may also forgive you your [own] failings and shortcomings and let them drop.

26 But if you do not forgive, neither will your Father in heaven forgive your failings and shortcomings.

As I said, Jesus' teaching didn't end with verse 24, where He said, in effect, "When you pray, believe you receive the things you desire, and you shall have them." Verse 25 begins with the word "and," a conjunction that links verse 24 to verse 25: *"AND when ye stand praying, FORGIVE. . . . "* Jesus was saying, "When you pray, believe you receive the things you desire, and you shall have them. *And* when you pray, forgive if you have anything against anyone. . . ."

Why did Jesus say this? He said it because *offense— holding a grudge or unforgiveness in your heart—will keep "the faith of God" from working in your life.* But when we learn how to forgive according to Mark 11:25–26, verses 23 and 24 will surely come to pass in our lives!

Forgive and Be Forgiven

In verse 26, Jesus said, *"But if ye do not forgive, NEITHER WILL YOUR FATHER WHICH IS IN HEAVEN FORGIVE YOUR TRESPASSES."* Friend, unforgiveness is serious business! We need to forgive so that our Heavenly Father can forgive *us*!

Someone said, "I don't know if I can accept that. It seems so harsh."

I want you to notice that Jesus was not talking to pagans when He said, "If you do not forgive others, your Father in Heaven will not forgive *you*." He was speaking to His disciples—His followers! That means He's talking to us too!

Are you a follower of God? If so, Jesus is saying to you, as He said to His early followers, "If you do not forgive others, your Father in Heaven will not forgive *you*." Since Mark 11:23–24 belongs to us, we must "own" Mark 11:25–26 too!

Also notice that the teaching in Mark 11:25–26 is not an isolated teaching from an isolated passage of Scripture. Not only do these verses about forgiveness fit the context, they can be substantiated by other passages. And, as we will see, love and forgiveness are attributes of a merciful God, whom we should follow closely and desire to imitate (Eph. 5:1).

For example, look at Matthew 6:14–15.

MATTHEW 6:14–15 (NIV)

14 For if you forgive men when they sin against you, your heavenly Father will also forgive you.

15 But if you do not forgive men their sins, your Father will not forgive your sins.

You might recognize these words of the Master as the teaching that followed what we commonly call The Lord's Prayer. After Jesus had taught the people how *not* to pray, He said in Matthew 6:9, *"This, then, is how you should pray . . ."* (NIV). Jesus proceeded to show them how to approach the Father. Then in verse 12, He said, *"Forgive us our debts, as we also have forgiven our debtors"* (NIV). The *Weymouth New Testament* says, *"Forgive us our shortcomings, as we also have forgiven those who have failed in their duty towards us."*

So although the settings are different, the words spoken by Jesus in Matthew 6:14–15 coincide with His words in Mark 11:25–26. In fact, in both passages, Jesus is literally saying the same thing: We must *forgive*!

Seeing Others in the Light of Christ

This command to forgive others and let go of offenses is not some far-fetched concept or theory that ministers have concocted just to annoy people! Certainly, some ministers have been guilty at times of taking one or two verses out of context to support their own ideas and beliefs. But I think you can see that the need to forgive others and to let go of offenses is an established truth.

A well-known story in Matthew chapter 18 further bears out this important fact.

MATTHEW 18:23–35 (NIV)

23 "Therefore, the kingdom of heaven is like a king who wanted to settle accounts with his servants.

24 As he began the settlement, a man who owed him ten thousand talents was brought to him.

25 Since he was not able to pay, the master ordered that he and his wife and his children and all that he had be sold to repay the debt.

26 The servant fell on his knees before him. 'Be patient with me,' he begged, 'and I will pay back everything.'

27 The servant's master took pity on him, canceled the debt and let him go.

28 But when that servant went out, he found one of his fellow servants who owed him a hundred denarii. He grabbed him and began to choke him. 'Pay back what you owe me!' he demanded.

29 His fellow servant fell to his knees and begged him, 'Be patient with me, and I will pay you back.'

30 But he refused. Instead, he went off and had the man thrown into prison until he could pay the debt.

31 When the other servants saw what had happened, they were greatly distressed and went and told their master everything that had happened.

32 Then the master called the servant in. 'You wicked servant,' he said, 'I canceled all that debt of yours because you begged me to.

33 Shouldn't you have had mercy on your fellow-servant just as I had on you?'

34 In anger his master turned him over to the jailers to be tortured, until he should pay back all he owed.

35 This is how my heavenly Father will treat each of you unless you forgive your brother from your heart."

Verse 33 in this passage is a key. It says, *"Shouldn't you have had mercy on your fellow-servant just as I had on you?'"* The king had forgiven this man of an impossible, insurmountable debt, yet the man turned around and demanded that a fellow servant repay him just a small debt in comparison.

Do you see the irony in this allegory? The king had forgiven that servant a debt of millions! Yet the same servant who was forgiven became merciless as he attempted to collect repayment of just a fraction of that amount from a fellow debtor.

God has forgiven each one of us an impossible debt. Therefore, Jesus wants us to know that no matter what others have done to us—no matter how deep the "debt" or offense—we must forgive them as God has forgiven us.

It's just this simple: If we're going to walk in the *faith* of God—the kind of faith Jesus talked about in Mark 11:23–24—we're going to have to walk in the *love* of God. In other words, if we're going to use the God-kind of faith as Jesus did when He cursed the fig tree, we're going to have to forgive as God forgives!

How God Forgives

How does God forgive? God loved mankind enough to give us His Son so that through Him we might be completely pardoned from the debt of sin, which we could not repay. God remitted our sin in Christ and made us new creations in Him (2 Cor. 5:17). And as children of God, if we miss it and sin, God forgives us when we ask Him to forgive us, and He cleanses us from all unrighteousness (1 John 1:9). That means He puts us back in right-standing with Himself as if we never did anything wrong.

Once God has forgiven us, the Bible says He remembers our sin no more (Isa. 43:25). He doesn't look at us in the light of what we did wrong. Instead, He sees us in the light of Christ—of who we are in Him.

God our Father wouldn't require something of us, His children, that He wasn't willing to do Himself. For example, God commands us to love as He loves and to forgive as He forgives. And as we've seen from Scripture, God loves deeply and forgives freely.

A good leader will never ask those under his leadership to do something he wouldn't do or be willing to do himself. At the ministry here in Tulsa, our employees and volunteers work hard, and my wife, Lynette, and I work hard too. Since this ministry began, I've done seemingly a little of everything—worked on cars, maintained the grounds, nailed up trim, installed sheetrock, and organized Bible school curriculum. Today, I administrate an international ministry and pastor a large local congregation.

Lynette and I have worked long hours doing hospital visitation, marriage counseling, and whatever was needed for the sake of the ministry, the Kingdom of God, and *people*. That's why we can ask others under our leadership to do the same.

Similarly, God would be unjust to ask us to forgive others if He wasn't willing to forgive, too, no matter what the offense. And since He is a just God, not only can He require us to forgive, He gives us the ability to do it!

'Forgive and Forget? Is That Really in the Bible?'

Over the years, I've heard many people say, "I know the Bible says we're to forgive, and I forgive So-and-so, all right. But I will *never* forget what he did to me!"

If you're still constantly thinking about what someone else did to you, you haven't forgiven him or her. To hold in memory someone's trespass or offense is not forgiving him! When you forgive someone of his or her wrongdoing, you have to "*. . . let it drop [leave it, let it go] . . .* " (Mark 11:25

Amplified) as the Scripture commands. In other words, you have to *forget* it.

I'm not saying that when you forgive someone, the person's offense will be completely erased from your memory. I'm saying that when thoughts return to your mind concerning the person's offense, you will choose not to dwell on those negative thoughts. You won't meditate or "camp out" on what he or she did wrong. You'll resist those wrong thoughts the same way you would resist any other kind of temptation to sin—as an act of your will and by faith.

Many of us have studied faith for so long that we should be well-versed in the process of "believing in our heart and confessing with our mouth" concerning God's promises. But have we spent any time meditating on scriptures about love and forgiveness? If we will hide God's Word in our heart concerning His mercy and then speak that Word when we're tempted to become offended, we won't have nearly as difficult a time walking in forgiveness. That means we'll forgive *and* forget—letting the offense go completely!

When you mention the subject of forgiving and forgetting, some people will immediately protest, "Yes, but you just don't know what that person did! You have no idea what I've been through!"

I don't have to know the details of the offense before I can point someone who's hurting to the Word of God and to the love of our gracious Heavenly Father. In every-thing—in every situation and circumstance—we should ask ourselves, *What does the Word say?* and *What would love do?*

The Desire for Revenge: An Unscriptural Attitude

Some people become so offended when they're wronged that they will wait with glee for some kind of judgment to be reckoned against their offender. They may even try to exact judgment on the offender themselves! When they're offended, they become proud, saying, "I'm not going to let him make a fool of me and get away with it!"

Or those who have been offended will say something such as, "Just wait—every dog has its day." What they really mean is, "My time will come when I'll get even." Then they wait for the right opportunity to pounce and get their revenge!

Friend, that kind of attitude is unscriptural. What's sad is that some of those same people will in the next breath say something such as, "I confess that God will meet all of my needs!" Often they don't see where they're missing it. They don't see that they're coming in line with God's Word in one area, but they're going completely against His Word in another area!

Some people refuse to forgive others because they think that forgiving them is the same as accepting that what they did wasn't wrong or that what they did wasn't "too terribly bad."

But, no, if someone hasn't really wronged you, why would God ask you to forgive the person? He wouldn't! You forgive *because* someone did something wrong!

When You Truly Forgive, You Won't Bring Up the Past

People make mistakes. I've made mistakes and so have you. And I bet you know people who, no matter how many times repentance has occurred, wouldn't let go of some wrongdoing. They wouldn't forgive and forget. But if you asked God to forgive you, He did. And if you were sincere, He will treat you as if you never committed sin. He will see you in the light of Christ.

Some people simply refuse to let go of the offenses of others. I have heard people talking about mistakes another person made 25 years ago! Yet they talk about them as if they happened yesterday! The person they're talking about may have asked God for forgiveness and may be living wholeheartedly for Him. God could be blessing that person, increasing and promoting him. But in the mind of those who refuse to let go of the grudge they're holding, the person is still steeped in sin.

Mercy Is Greater Than Judgment

Too many people, including Christians, want justice instead of mercy when someone else has sinned— especially if the person sinned against *them*! They think only in terms of the offender "getting what's coming to him"—that is, until *they* need mercy. Then they want mercy and not judgment!

I'm not talking about someone who has broken the laws of the land and must face penalties in our criminal court system. Certainly, God's mercy can operate in those cases if the person who committed the crime is genuinely repentant. He or she could receive a lesser sentence or receive some other manifestation of mercy.

However, our justice system was put in place for a good reason, and the Bible talks strongly about obeying "governing authorities" (see Rom. 13:1–6). Still, if someone is facing the pronouncement of some penalty or sentence from one of these authorities, our attitude toward that person, for whom Christ died, should be one of mercy, not condemnation.

People who think only in terms of judgment when someone misses it don't understand the fact that we all deserve judgment. The Bible says, ". . . *ALL have sinned, and come short of the glory of God"* (Rom. 3:23). But God forgave us in Christ. Second Corinthians 5:19 says, *". . . God was in Christ, reconciling the world unto himself, NOT IMPUTING THEIR TRESPASSES UNTO THEM; and hath committed unto us the word of reconciliation."*

So we were all deserving of eternal judgment. But God in Christ reconciled us to Himself, and those who accept the sacrifice of Christ become recipients of God's mercy, which is *far greater* than judgment.

LUKE 6:37 (Amplified)

37 Judge not [neither pronouncing judgment nor subjecting to censure], and you will not be judged; do not condemn and pronounce guilty, and you will not be condemned and pronounced guilty; acquit and forgive

and release (give up resentment, let it drop), and you will be acquitted and forgiven and released.

In general, we don't like to hear this sort of teaching, because it sometimes confronts us with a need to change. Our flesh, especially when we're dealing with offense, would rather do things *its* way than *God's* way.

The flesh likes having its own set of rules to live by, such as, "If you get me, I'll get you back," or, "I don't get mad; I get even," or, "I don't get even—I get *ahead*!" But as believers in God and His Word, we are responsible to bring ourselves in line with the Word—spirit, soul, and body. That's not always easy to do. In fact, it's hard on the flesh to do what God says to do, especially when we're offended or we're used to letting our flesh have its own way.

You know, no one else can obey God for you. No one but you can forgive if you have something against someone else. I can't forgive that person for you—and your spouse, parent, sibling, cousin, friend, or co-worker can't do it for you! Only *you* can hunker down with the Word of God and make a rock-hard decision to forgive, come what may! But I promise you, no matter how difficult it is to forgive and no matter how many times you fall back into patterns of unforgiveness from the past, if you will stay with the Word, the Word will stay with you and reward you in ways you never dreamed possible.

The bitter consequences of allowing offense to remain in our lives are too great, as we will look at in greater detail in the following chapter. If we permit offense to darken our hearts and minds and refuse to deal with it, we will eventually shut ourselves off completely from the blessings of God.

The benefits of refusing offense are also great. If you will refuse to permit the least bit of unforgiveness in your heart, you will open yourself up for the rich treasures of Heaven to be manifested in your life, and you'll become a blessing to many others besides.

So I ask you, why *fail* in life when you can *forgive*?

Chapter 2

The High Cost of Offense

Many in the Body of Christ have given the world ammunition with which to attack Christianity. Some outside of Christ are so harsh in their criticism of the Church because of the wrong example many Christians have set for them. Jesus said, *"By THIS shall all men know that ye are my disciples, IF YE HAVE LOVE ONE TO ANOTHER"* (John 13:35). Yet the world has witnessed believers striving, lying, backbiting, and being offended one against another.

The world is not impressed with our confessions of faith and our whooping and hollering about the faith message when they see us mistreat our brothers and sisters in the Lord. Certainly, we *should* be excited about the message of faith and about God meeting our needs and our desires.

The world needs to see our enthusiasm about the things of God—about being blessed and being a blessing to others.

However, all the excitement in the world is no substitute for a genuine faith in God's Word that's born of love. When we're manifesting the fruit of the Spirit, and the Word of God is producing something in our lives, people will notice. And they will stop accusing us of living in "la-la land" and calling that faith.

Offense Will Choke the Life of the Word From Your Heart

Often a person doesn't see the great harm he does to himself when he bitterly holds on to a grudge against someone. He doesn't see it because the effects of his sin don't just manifest instantly or overnight. They begin slowly and subtly, and they build up inside him until he is overcome with bitterness and becomes almost a different person.

I sometimes liken holding a grudge to a person allowing cholesterol to build up in his arteries. Cholesterol builds in the arteries bit by bit until they are completely blocked, and blood ceases to flow through those vessels.

Notice the person's arteries do not start out blocked. They begin with just a little bit of cholesterol attaching itself to the vessel walls, which "attracts" more and more cholesterol. By the time it is discovered, the damage is oftentimes beyond repair.

Similarly, just a "little" grudge that you refuse or neglect to deal with can fester and become bigger and bigger until it cuts off the flow of the Spirit of life within. I'm not saying that a Christian who holds a grudge loses his salvation; I'm simply saying he walks and lives as one who isn't born again because he cuts himself off from the flow of life, blessing, and favor that he should be enjoying.

Also, have you ever noticed that a person who won't forgive not only loses his peace and his joy, but he ceases to walk in the light in other ways too? A person who's been offended and hasn't dealt with it scripturally often becomes confused in his thinking. He becomes vulnerable to embracing strange teachings that cause him to err further and further from paths of righteousness.

And it's no wonder. If we're not walking in the *love* of God, we're not walking in the *light* of God. Instead, we're walking in the darkness of Satan, sin, and the world. But Psalm 36:9 says, *". . . with thee* [Lord] *is the fountain of life: in thy light shall we see light."* When we walk in the love and light of God, we can see the light.

Don't Let Offense Jeopardize Your Future

Years ago, there was a certain young student at RHEMA Bible Training Center who approached me, desperate because his world was falling apart around him. In talking with me, he revealed that his roommate had moved out of the apartment the two students had shared, and since this young man couldn't financially keep the apartment without a roommate, he had to make other living arrangements. It meant his having to move into a smaller apartment that was not as nice as the one he had lived in. In fact, he called his new apartment a "dump."

As he shared his story, I could tell that this student was angry and offended that his roommate had moved. The two men had verbally agreed to rent the nicer apartment together for the duration of the school year. But when the six-month lease was due to expire, the roommate gave this young man two months' notice that he was going to move out on his own into another apartment.

After talking to me at some length, the young man finally blurted out, "He didn't live up to his end of the bargain. *He did me wrong!*"

I did my best to encourage this student to put the incident behind him and to move on with his life and with what God had in store for him in his studies and in ministry. In fact, I *strongly* encouraged him. He had become so angry at one point that I just bluntly said, "Look, son, you'd better let this thing go, or it's going to ruin your entire life."

Within just a short period of time—with only about a month left in the school year—the dean of students had to expel this young man. Despite all our best efforts to work with this student, his behavior became so bizarre and erratic that we had no choice except to let him go.

At that time, the student dress code at RHEMA required men to wear slacks, dress shirts, and neckties. Yet this young man began showing up to class in jeans and T-shirts! What's worse, each time he was confronted, he refused to change. He'd leave the campus, shouting things such as, "This is a free country. I can wear what I want!"

During one particular incident, one of our faculty members gently tried to explain to the young man his obligation to abide by the school's rules that had been set forth in the student handbook. The young student argued, "So what! Show me that rule in the Bible!"

The faculty member wisely replied, "Well, there's nothing in the Bible that says I have to have a driver's license to drive. But if I get caught driving without one, I am going to suffer the consequences nevertheless."

Parts of this story might be comical if the situation weren't so sad. The young man refused to change. Although he had been a promising student who had earned very good grades in school, his life began to unravel because he allowed the enemy a stronghold in his life through offense. The bitterness in his heart affected his education, his job, many of his relationships—*his whole life*—all because he wouldn't forgive.

Robbery in Progress

In my almost 70 years of living, I have seen offense run its ugly course in people's lives time and time again, stealing from them their spirituality, their relationships, their finances, and their health. Not only that, but when someone harbors an offense, it's like a robbery in progress to those around him as well.

I have also observed offenses ranging from some grave offense to something as petty as someone arriving late to church and finding another person sitting in "his" pew! I have actually seen people turn around and leave a church service because someone else sat where they usually sit in the church on Sunday morning! I've also seen churches so divided that two groups will start a feud, and one group will sit on one side of the church, and the other group will sit on the other side—and the two sides will *never* cross!

I'm thinking of one such example as I write. Many years ago, this particular church had already been divided on some frivolous issue. There were two main groups that opposed each other, and they all sat opposite one another in the church to let everyone know it! They began feuding again when the pastor chose someone from group "A" to play the piano in church, and he chose a worship leader from among group "B"!

So a member from one group played the piano on the platform alongside the worship leader, who was from the other group. Then the poor pastor had to get up and minister after this so-called team tried to lead the congregation into the worship of a holy God!

Offense started this church rift, and offense perpetuated it. I don't know the outcome of this particular feud, but I know from my general observations over the years that unless peace is made and the conflict resolved, a church that is split in this manner will eventually die.

You Have Nothing to Gain and Everything to Lose by Becoming Offended

It's been said that in life, nothing is free. If that adage is referring to sowing and reaping or even to "cause and effect," it could certainly hold true. In other words, there will always be consequences to the choices we make. And especially in the case of offense, there is a tremendously high price tag attached to our allowing it to remain in our lives.

If you allow offense to remain in your life, it will hinder your creativity and hamper your ability to perform your job or ministry. Offense can shut doors of opportunity for promotion. It will hinder your spiritual progress and your walk with the Lord and will keep you from receiving all that He has for you. Harboring offense will spiritually bankrupt you.

There's a definite price to pay spiritually for harboring offense, as we've seen in Scripture. But let's look at how offense can devastate a person, naturally speaking.

A person who is easily offended, or who is constantly offended at one person or another, becomes a fighter. In other words, he becomes a person who fights his way through life, looking out for "number one." Instead of allowing God to work through him, he is constantly beating his own path, blazing his own trail, and fighting his way to where he wants to go. Others might describe his personality as "antagonistic"; it seems he is just looking for a fight. Not only is he easily offended, he readily offends others and often leaves a trail of broken relationships behind him.

Even believers who fall into offense's trap can't seem to follow peace because it's been so long since they've been in touch with the peace and the Presence of God. They often don't recognize the gentle wooing of the Holy Spirit when He tries to guide them in the right direction.

Often, going in the right direction and getting back on the right path means making amends in some relationships—something an offended person finds difficult to do. Rather than try to right some wrongs and walk a path that keeps getting brighter and brighter, he continues on a path of his own making, and his way becomes clouded and dark.

Some Important Questions to Ask

My father often said that he never prayed a prayer for himself that wasn't eventually answered. However, he taught that when he wasn't seeing answers to prayer after a period of time, the first place he would always look was at his love walk. He would ask himself the questions, *Am I holding a grudge? Am I harboring bitterness, ill will, or animosity toward anyone?* When he got those answers straight, he'd go back to what he was believing for and refuse to budge in his stand on God's Word.

Dad always said publicly, "I refuse to permit the least bit of ill will or animosity in my heart against anyone." (Notice he could either permit it or *refuse* to permit it; the choice was his.) And he lived his private life in the same manner. He told me at an early age, "Son, if you will refuse to take offense, you'll never be out of the will of God, and you'll never fail to receive the blessings of God."

There's a great lesson packed into that one small statement. Learning that lesson early has kept me from a lot of trouble that I would have otherwise fallen into headfirst!

When you're tempted to become offended, before you simply plunge headlong into deep bitterness and unforgiveness, stop and ask yourself these questions: *Is this where I want to get stuck in life? Are these the people I want to get stuck with? Is this the level of blessing I want to walk in, or do I want to go further with God?*

We need to ask ourselves these questions because harboring offense will harm us individually more than it will harm anyone else. Therefore, we must count the costs of harboring offense and weigh carefully the consequences. Will our harboring offense be worth the cost we will eventually have to pay? It's a good question that deserves our serious consideration.

It's been said that sin will take you further than you want to go, keep you longer than you want to stay, and cost you more than you want to pay. That is certainly true of the sin of offense. Offense will bring you needless suffering and cause you to say and do things you never would have thought about saying and doing before. Offense will lead you astray and deter you from your divine destiny. At worst, offense will cause you to miss the plans and purposes of God for your life altogether. It's much too high a price to pay.

Chapter 3

The 'Whys' of Offense

Most of us understand that offense is Satan's tool to distract us from God and His Word, rendering us incapable of bearing fruit spiritually and glorifying the Lord. (We will look at this topic in greater detail later in the book.) We hopefully also have the understanding that we should avoid this deadly enemy of offense at all costs.

In this chapter we're going to look at some of the causes of offense and why it occurs. Knowing what causes offense will help us avoid it when the opportunity to become offended comes our way.

'Me, Myself, and I'—A Question of Focus

One of the big reasons people become offended is because they are too self-focused. Instead of focusing on the Word or on helping others, they are focused on themselves and *their* needs, *their* lack, *their* wounds, *their* pain, and so forth.

People like this are always thinking about the injustices committed against them and, in general, feel life hasn't been fair to them. They carry the injustices of the past like a badge of honor, unaware that they're not living in the present where God wants them to live, and they're not where they should be spiritually.

Someone once said, "I know people in the world like that who harbor grudges for months or even years. But Christians would never do that!" On the contrary, this self-pitying attitude has found its way inside the four walls of the Church. And not only does offense stop the flow of God's blessing in the life of the individual who harbors the grudge, it can also short-circuit the power of God among a local assembly of believers.

Offenses usually take hold of us because of the people each of us tends to love the most: *me, myself,* and *I*! In other words, when our focus becomes skewed so that we're thinking only of ourselves, we become prime targets for offense to occur in our lives. Then once we do become offended, *"me, myself, and I"* become the focus of our lives to an even greater degree!

People usually become offended and *stay* offended when they're thinking predominantly of themselves and what will benefit *them*. What's ironic about that kind of mentality is, in focusing only on what they think is best for them, they lose sight of the will of God for their lives.

Has anyone ever said to you, "Don't worry—I've got your back"? God has our best interests at heart more than anyone else does. He "has our back"! And God is the only One who knows what's best for us. But when we become offended, we lose focus of all that. All we can see is how we've been wronged. We become very *self*-focused.

People who become easily offended have little or no consciousness of other people's needs. Consequently, they are not very servant-minded. They become weak in Christian service, because they are too busy focusing on what's most important to them—*themselves*! They become so self-focused that they are clueless concerning the needs of the world around them.

The Hidden Motive of Jealousy

Many times, people become offended because of jealousy. We don't always recognize this sly culprit, because if someone is giving place to jealousy in his life, he usually doesn't want to admit it; he would rather keep it hidden.

Jealousy manifests itself in all kinds of ways. People who try to promote themselves or who try to jockey for a position are often motivated by jealousy. If you don't believe it, just watch how offended they become if someone else receives the promotion instead! You could point the finger at a person like this and say, "You're just jealous," and most of the time, he or she will flatly deny it.

Have you ever believed God for something over a period of time and then witnessed someone else ask God for the same thing and receive it almost immediately? If so, were you tempted to be offended or unhappy that the other person received his or her answer? If you fail to shake off, or *fling* from you, those wrong feelings and attitudes, they will end up getting the best of you and robbing you of the blessings God intends for you to have.

A Devoted Shepherd and a Jealous King

Let's look at two men in the Bible, David and Saul, who each had the opportunity to become offended. One man succumbed to offense; the other did not. They each experienced very different outcomes as a result of their choices.

1 SAMUEL 18:6–11 (NKJV)

6 Now it had happened as they were coming home, when David was returning from the slaughter of the Philistine, that the women had come out of all the cities of Israel, singing and dancing, to meet King Saul, with tambourines, with joy, and with musical instruments.

7 So the women sang as they danced, and said: "Saul has slain his thousands, And David his ten thousands."

8 Then Saul was very angry, and the saying displeased him; and he said, "They have ascribed to David ten thousands, and to me they have ascribed only thousands. Now what more can he have but the kingdom?"

9 So Saul eyed David [with a jealous eye] from that day forward.

10 And it happened on the next day that the distressing spirit from God came upon Saul, and he prophesied inside the house. So David played music with his hand, as at other times; but there was a spear in Saul's hand.

11 And Saul cast the spear, for he said, "I will pin David to the wall!" But David escaped his presence twice.

Jealousy was at the root of King Saul's offense against David. Because of David's defeat of the giant, he had been promoted from the rank of lowly shepherd boy to a commander in Saul's army. David's only "crime" was his faith in God and his giftedness in battle, yet Saul hated him.

When David returned from routing the Philistines in battle, women were singing songs about him and his cunning military feats. Saul heard it and chose offense. The people ascribed praise to David for his acts of heroism, and Saul didn't like it. Because the people didn't herald Saul as "number one" in the land, he became jealous, angry, and offended.

Saul's life from that point forward illustrates the sinister progression of offense if it is not dealt with. When Saul became offended at David, Saul's focus turned to David. Instead of looking to the Lord for wisdom to lead His people, Saul became totally consumed—obsessed—with removing David from the picture.

First, Saul tried repeatedly to kill David. Then he became offended at his own son for defending David, his declared rival and enemy.

1 SAMUEL 20:30–33 (NKJV)

30 Then Saul's anger was aroused against Jonathan, and he said to him, "You son of a perverse, rebellious woman! Do I not know that you have chosen the son of Jesse [David] to your own shame and to the shame of your mother's nakedness?

31 "For as long as the son of Jesse lives on the earth, you shall not be established, nor your kingdom. Now therefore, send and bring him to me, for he shall surely die."

32 And Jonathan answered Saul his father, and said to him, "Why should he be killed? What has he done?"

33 Then Saul cast a spear at him to kill him, by which Jonathan knew that it was determined by his father to kill David.

Much later, in the heat of battle, Saul took his own life, thus ending the sad reign of a man chosen by God to lead His people. Disobedience, and later, jealousy and offense, had taken Saul far from the path of one fulfilling his divine destiny.

1 SAMUEL 31:4 (NKJV)

4 Then Saul said to his armorbearer, "Draw your sword, and thrust me through with it, lest these uncircumcised men come and thrust me through and abuse me." But his armorbearer would not, for he was greatly afraid. Therefore Saul took a sword and fell on it.

Saul had lost the anointing to be king of Israel due to his own disobedience, *not* David's great military prowess (see 1 Sam. 15:1–23). From that point on, Saul spiraled downward spiritually and became a deeply troubled man. And we know that both his reign and his own life ended in dishonor.

Now let's look at how David chose to handle offense when the opportunity presented itself to him to become offended.

1 SAMUEL 24:10–12 (NKJV)

10 "Look, this day your eyes have seen that the Lord delivered you today into my hand in the cave, and someone urged me to kill you. But my eye spared you, and I said, 'I will not stretch out my hand against my lord, for he is the Lord's anointed.'

11 "Moreover, my father, see! [David was talking to King Saul here.] Yes, see the corner of your robe in my hand! For in that I cut off the corner of your robe, and did not kill you, know and see that there is neither evil nor rebellion in my hand, and I have not sinned against you. Yet you hunt my life to take it.

12 "Let the Lord judge between you and me, and let the Lord avenge me on you. But my hand shall not be against you.

David stood on the other side of the gorge from where Saul lay sleeping and yelled over to him. Then David held up a piece of Saul's robe, which he had cut off while Saul was fast asleep. David let Saul know that he could have killed him. But David chose to take the high road. He said, in essence, "You choose to hunt me down to kill me, but I choose to walk in love."

David could have become offended that Saul was trying to kill him! David certainly had his opportunity to demand or execute revenge. But David feared God and would not *"touch God's anointed"* (1 Chron. 16:22), although God had already stripped the kingdom from Saul because of his disobedience.

Two Different Choices— Two Very Different Outcomes

We already know Saul's end—the sad results of his choices. What about David? We read in the Bible that David enjoyed God's protection and eventually took his place as king. David lived in the blessings of God because he chose not to be distracted by offense.

Saul died on his own sword as a result of taking offense. David became king in Saul's stead as a result of refusing offense. Saul died in mid-life; David lived to a ripe old age. Saul had become hardheaded and stiff-necked, rebelling against the commands of God. David remained tenderhearted, and although he made some grave mistakes later in life, he repented, and God called David a man after His own heart (Acts 13:22), because David was quick to repent. Saul fell short of accomplishing the will of God for his life. However, David fulfilled God's plan for his life because of his tough choice to focus on God and His will instead of on the many offenses committed against him.

We also know God protected David, because with Saul's military experience, I'm sure he was an expert with the javelin. Under ordinary circumstances, Saul should have been able to pin someone to the wall with his spear! However, time and again, David evaded Saul's attempts to kill him.

I wonder how many of us would have reacted the way David did if we were being hunted down like a wild animal! If we were constantly fleeing for our life and had an opportunity to end our ordeal, would we plunge our sword into our enemy as he slept?

I can just imagine David's men standing by as David was faced with his decision. No doubt at least some of them were saying, "Go ahead, David. That man is crazy, and he's wearing us all out. Put a stop to this right now!"

Yet David cut only a portion of Saul's robe and walked away. David showed real humility, reverence, and trust before God. But how many people today would become so offended that they would spitefully *annihilate* their enemy if they thought they could get away with it! We don't see enough believers in our day having the attitude, "Lord, You be the Judge. I refuse to take offense."

My Own Choice to Refuse Offense

In my younger days, I was so highly competitive that if you said anything negative about me or my family, I wanted to take matters into my own hands right then and do something about it! I had an uncle—Uncle Dub Hagin—who was the same way. (Before he passed away, there were times I wanted to call on Uncle Dub to come help me fight!)

It's difficult not to take offense when people call you heretics and come against you via television, radio, and books, ridiculing you because of your faith. But by the grace of God, neither my dad, nor I, nor my son Craig has ever retaliated in any fashion.

People might forget over time what someone wrote or said about you. But it would take them longer to forget it if you reacted in the flesh, returning "evil for evil." The Bible says, *"Do not take revenge, my friends, but leave room for God's wrath, for it is written: 'It is mine to avenge; I will repay,' says the Lord"* (Rom. 12:19 NIV). He is the Judge—so we need to let Him judge! Then we simply need to continue on the path of obedience to His will, minding *His* business and refusing to be distracted.

Saul's Son Jonathan Refused to Be Offended

Now let's look at the life of Jonathan, the son of Saul. Jonathan was next in line to be king in Saul's stead. Jonathan could have become offended when the prophet Samuel anointed David as the next king of Israel. Yet Jonathan remained a friend to David his entire life. And because he refused to be offended, his son Mephibosheth inherited his blessings and the favor of David when David eventually became king.

2 SAMUEL 9:9–11 (NKJV)

9 And the king called to Ziba, Saul's servant, and said to him, "I have given to your master's son all that belonged to Saul and to all his house.

10 "You therefore, and your sons and your servants, shall work the land for him, and you shall bring in the harvest, that your master's son may have food to eat. But Mephibosheth your master's son shall eat bread at my table always." Now Ziba had fifteen sons and twenty servants.

11 Then Ziba said to the king, "According to all that my lord the king has commanded his servant, so will your servant do." "As for Mephibosheth," said the king, "he shall eat at my table like one of the king's sons."

According to history, when someone outside the lineage of the king, or someone other than the "heir apparent," took his place on the throne as the new king, the new leader often destroyed the entire family of the previous ruler lest someone in the lineage cause an uprising, usurp the king, and retake the throne. The new king would annihilate the family of the previous ruler and seize all of his possessions, including houses and lands.

But in David's case, he and Jonathan had made a covenant together to bless, not destroy, each other. Jonathan—heir to the throne in Saul's place—had died in battle, yet because of Jonathan's covenant friendship with David, the surviving descendant of Jonathan was blessed. Mephibosheth was treated as King David's own son because of the godly decision of Jonathan, his father, to refuse offense. (In a later chapter, we will cover in greater detail the power of refusal in dealing with offense.)

We should refuse offense in our lives if for no other reason than the blessing and well-being of our children! Too often we think that to let go of a suffered wrong is too big a price to pay. However, the opposite is true, as we have seen. Holding on to an offense carries with it a high price that could cost us as well as those we love.

Wrongs and Perceived Wrongs

Offense can occur when someone becomes focused on the wrong committed against him or on the wrong he *perceives* has been committed.

I understand some of the feelings of jealousy and perceived wrongs that can get the best of even the most dedicated Christians, including ministers. When I was a young preacher on a church staff as an associate pastor, I was asked by the pastor to minister to the congregation on a Sunday morning while he was out of town. When he returned, several of the people in the church told him, "The young man did a great job."

The people's intentions were good. They were just trying to put the pastor at ease, letting him know that everything went smoothly in his absence. However, from that time on, I never ministered to the people of that church again! Every time the pastor left town, he would invite a visiting speaker to fill in for him. Don't misunderstand me. Many of those visiting ministers did a great job ministering to the people. But I could preach better than some of them.

To this day, I don't know if perhaps that pastor thought I wanted to take his church away from him. I didn't want it! It was his church, and I respected that. I actually had no aspirations of ever becoming the senior pastor of that church. But for some reason or another, he became offended at me.

Not every perceived wrong is actually a wrong. Some people become offended over what they *think* is an injustice, because they misinterpret the situation, as in the case of that senior pastor. Others will become offended if someone tells them the truth about something they may need to change in their lives—even if that truth is spoken in a spirit of meekness and love.

Have you ever noticed that someone who doesn't want to hear the truth will become offended at the person who tells the truth—and then blame that person for offending him!

For example, I could say to a church member, "I'd really like to see you get more involved at church," and he or she could "blow up" or sulk about it, saying, "I attend services and pay my tithes. What right does he have to say such a thing to me!"

Offense works both ways between church laity and leadership. In other words, some pastors or leaders become offended because a volunteer doesn't do a particular job the way they think it should be done.

I have been in the ministry long enough to know that if I have willing, sincere people helping me, as long as they get the job done and the desired outcome is achieved, I shouldn't nitpick at their methods. Each of us is different. We each have different strengths, different methods of problem-solving, and different ways of accomplishing a goal. Therefore, we may each take slightly different routes to arrive at that goal or destination. The important thing is accomplishing the vision while developing people for Kingdom service over the long-haul—not picking apart their methodology.

Offense Comes Because of the Word

I could not consider this chapter complete without showing you in some detail the ultimate "why" of offense. *Offense comes for the sake of the Word*—to remove it from the heart of the believer so that he or she becomes incapable of bearing fruit and of receiving answers to prayer.

Jesus offered the following insight about those who become offended and cut themselves off from the Word in this manner.

MARK 4:16–17

16 And these are they likewise which are sown on stony ground; who, when they have heard the word, immediately receive it with gladness;

17 And have no root in themselves, and so endure but for a time: afterward, when affliction or persecution ariseth for the word's sake, immediately they are offended.

Here we see a certain kind of people—those who are prone to becoming offended. These people hear the Word with gladness, and for a period of time, they do all right. But then someone will say or do something that they don't like, and they become offended.

Some people are so easily offended, they can't even go to church on Sunday morning without finding something to get upset about: So-and-so didn't speak to them after the service; the pastor said something they didn't like; they didn't like the praise and worship; someone sat in their favorite seat in the sanctuary. The list could go on and on.

I don't know how many times over the years I have received phone calls or letters in which people have said, "Pastor walked past my pew on Sunday and didn't stop to visit with me. Is he mad at me? It really hurt my feelings."

These people weren't concerned that I didn't hold a conversation with the thousands of other people who attended the same service. They were only concerned that I didn't go out of my way to have a conversation with *them.*

Every week after the Sunday morning service, my wife and I go to one of the church's exits to shake hands with the people who leave through those doors. Each week, we go to a different exit on a rotating basis. There are four exits, so in a given month, we can potentially see every church member and shake his or her hand.

At the exits, I try to shake hands with and greet each person as he or she walks by, but I don't have time to stop and speak personally to anyone. I usually only have time to shake hands and say, "Hi" or, "It's good to see you." In other words, I can't stop and engage someone in conversation, because if I did that, I would miss shaking hands with others.

Before a service begins, I often walk past people who are already seated to get the attention of an usher or a staff member concerning some aspect of the service. I don't stop and greet everyone I see on the way, because I've got something else on my mind that I'm trying to take care of. Yet some people will get offended if I walk past their pew and don't stop to visit with them!

Let's look again at the characteristics of the people Jesus was talking about in Mark 4:16–17. It says, *". . . when they have heard the word, immediately receive it with gladness."* You've probably seen people who hear the Word and get so excited that they dance and shout. The people Jesus refers to in this passage are like that. They receive the Word with gladness; unfortunately, their joy is short-lived and lasts only for a season.

After a season of rejoicing over the Word of God, something will happen in the lives of these believers, and they will fall away from the Word. They were beginning to bear fruit, but something happened to halt their faith. Verse 17 calls it *affliction, tribulation,* or *persecution.* When pressure is applied, these believers don't have a solid root system that establishes them firmly on the truth.

Therefore, they are shaken by the trouble that arises, and they become *offended*.

We look at people who are exuberant about the Word of God and think they're the ones who are going to bear "much fruit" and glorify God (John 15:8). There's nothing wrong with getting excited about the Word, but just getting excited about it isn't evidence enough that someone is established on God's Word and steadfast in faith. We just saw in Mark 4:16–17 that just the opposite could be true: A person could receive the Word with gladness, yet have no root system that sustains his or her faith when the pressures, tests, and storms of life arise.

Psalm 119:165

165 Great peace have they which love thy law: and nothing shall offend them.

If you're really grounded in the Word, nothing will offend you. I'm not saying that nothing will ever come your way to offend you. I'm simply saying that you will recognize and refuse offense when it comes. You'll walk over the top of offense, and you'll keep on walking. You will say as Jesus said, *"Lord forgive them. They know not what they do."*

Have you ever heard the phrase "standing in faith" or "standing your ground in faith"? Ephesians 6:13 says,

"Therefore put on the full armour of God, so that when the day of evil comes, you may be able to stand your ground, and after you have done everything, to stand" (NIV).

When a person is standing his ground in faith for some answer to prayer, the picture is of a person who is *standing firm,* who is *fixed* or *set,* and who is *immovable.* But if that same person gives way to offense, he would cease to remain *firm, fixed, set,* and *immovable.* He would lose his footing and stumble, or waver, in his faith.

Friend, offense will steal from you your spiritual stability—your ability to endure in tough times. Your ability to stand your ground amidst the winds of adversity is crucial to your receiving from God and walking in His highest and best. Can you see why, when you've been offended, God says to *"forgive him and let it drop (leave it, let it go)"*? (See Mark 11:25 Amplified.)

Let's continue looking at the type of person Jesus was talking about in Mark 4:16–17 who *receives the Word with gladness, endures for a time,* but then *becomes offended.*

MARK 4:16–17

16 And these are they likewise which are sown on stony ground; who, when they have heard the word, immediately receive it with gladness;

17 And have no root in themselves, and so endure but for a time: afterward, when affliction or persecution ariseth for the word's sake, immediately they are offended.

Affliction and persecution are ways in which Satan will try to make you offended. And he especially loves it when a believer becomes offended at God. For example, a believer might receive the Word of God with joy. But after a time, when trouble comes near but the answer seems far away, he will say something such as, "Well, I thought I was in the will of God, but I guess I'm not. It looks like He's forgotten me."

Whether a person who does this will admit it or not, he is offended. God hasn't done what the person thought He should have done. Things aren't turning out the way the person thought they should. So now he is upset and ready to give up and quit. He is *offended*.

If you're going to follow the plan of God for your life, you *will* be persecuted! Instead of looking at persecution as a sign you're doing something *wrong*, you might try looking at it as a sign you're doing something *right*! Yet how many people play right into the enemy's hands and allow discouragement to cause them to lose their footing and fall from their place of standing?

As I said, when we fail to receive from God, the problem is never with God. *"God is not a man that He should lie"* (Num. 23:19). He is completely faithful to perform that which He has promised. So if we've asked for something He has plainly provided in His Word, He is not withholding that blessing from us. But there are things we can do to hinder ourselves from receiving from Him. He wants us to receive the blessing, but we often take ourselves out of position to receive.

By way of illustration, if you were to turn on a shower and step inside too far to the left or right of the flow of water streaming down, you're not going to benefit from that shower as much as you would if you were standing directly underneath the water's flow. If you want to get wet, you're going to have to position yourself in line with the stream of water!

Similarly, if you want to receive God's blessings, you're going to have to position yourself in line with the Word. Remember, if we want to receive what God wants us to have, we need to find out how He works and work with Him.

Many people remove themselves from a position of receiving from God and then become resentful at Him because they're not being blessed in life as they think they should be. How does a person get out of position for receiving blessing? One big way is through offense.

Let's look at a phrase in Mark 4:17.

MARK 4:17

17 And have no root in themselves, and so endure but for a time; afterward, when affliction or persecution ariseth FOR THE WORD'S SAKE, immediately they are offended.

When we're going through a particularly difficult test or trial, most of us will at some point at least have the thought, *Why, Lord? Why is this happening to me?* This verse tells us why we suffer affliction when we're standing on the Word. *Affliction and persecution come for the sake of the Word!*

The enemy doesn't bring offense your way because you're someone special! No, he does it because he wants to steal the Word from you that's been sown in your heart. If he can steal the Word from you through offense, he can steal your blessing. If he can steal your blessing, he can steal your fruitfulness. And if he can cause you to be barren and unfruitful in your knowledge of the Word, he can destroy you.

On the other hand, if Satan can't get you to succumb to offense or give up on God's Word, he can't steal from you what the Word promises you. He can't have your salvation, your healing, your prosperity, your family—your answers to prayer!

The enemy is jubilant when he hears believers say things such as, "I'm so mad—I'm never going back to that church again!" or, "I tried that faith stuff, and it didn't work. God didn't come through for me. I'm *through* believing His Word," or, "Everyone at my church is mad at me because I went to a healing revival. I don't think I want to delve into the truth concerning healing. I'm never going to another healing service *ever.*"

I don't understand why some Christians will do just about anything to keep someone from criticizing or persecuting them. It's almost as if they think that if someone is coming against them, they must be doing something wrong. What they fail to realize is, the reason someone is coming against them could well be that they are doing something *right*!

It has been a challenge, but I have learned over the years not to care what others think of me. People have said to me at various times over the years, "Did you know that So-and-so wrote a book and said such-and-such about you?"

"Yes, I know," I reply.

"Well, doesn't it bother you that he said all those things?" they ask. "Aren't you going to do something about it?"

"No, I'm not going to do a thing about it," is always my response. You see, I don't have to defend myself when I'm striving to obey God and to do what pleases Him. God said that He would defend me. So my attitude can genuinely be, *Father, forgive them, for they know not what they do.*

I have learned that when you're really doing something for God, persecution just comes with the territory! You don't have to go looking for persecution. You don't even have to do anything extraordinary to receive it. All you have to do is obey God, and sooner or later, trouble will rear its ugly head against you. Why? I think it's because some people don't like it when others are successful.

When I see someone who's successful in his or her respective field, I don't try to make trouble for that person. Instead, I want to learn from that person. Yet some people will tease and taunt the person who finds success in his or her chosen field. They are offended at others' success. Then they wonder why *they* never succeed at anything!

Could it be that they're using time being critical that they could be using to make themselves better?

Have you ever heard the saying, "You can't light your own candle by putting someone else's candle out"? In other words, putting others down doesn't improve you—neither does it make you look any better. You look better in the eyes of most people when you're putting something into others instead of tearing them down. And you get better at whatever it is you do in life by improving yourself, not criticizing others.

So if you see other Christians succeeding, and you are not finding the success you desire, don't get upset with them. Don't bad-mouth them. Instead, look at what they're doing right and at what you may be doing wrong. Be confident that God is truly no respecter of persons. He will bless you just as He'll bless any of His children if you'll just walk with Him and His Word and steer clear of offense.

Several years ago during the Charismatic Renewal, it seemed believers were receiving the baptism in the Holy Spirit in droves. In one particular meeting, some old-time Pentecostals, who'd been saved for years and who'd been taught to tarry in order to receive from God, became upset because so many "newcomers" in the faith were getting filled with the Spirit.

One dear gentleman said, "I just don't understand all these people getting filled with the Holy Ghost, and God is blessing them. Yet I've been saved and have been serving God all these years, and I'm getting *nothing*!"

This man didn't know that the baptism in the Holy Spirit belonged to him just as much as it belonged to any other believer. So instead of rejoicing with others who were being blessed, he became offended. He thought God was withholding from Him, but in reality, he was talking himself out of receiving from God.

Do you want to know how to guarantee yourself the same kind of blessing someone else receives? When you hear of someone receiving a blessing, *rejoice* with him! The Bible says we are to rejoice with those who rejoice (Rom. 12:15).

So if you're believing God for a new car, and someone you know gets a new car, *rejoice* with that person! Doing so will put you in position to receive the same kind of blessing, but becoming offended will take you out of position to receive from God.

We Receive From God With a Good and Honest Heart

We looked at the verse that says, *"Great peace have they which love thy law: and nothing shall offend them"* (Ps. 119:165). People who continually feed on the Word, reading and meditating on it, aren't easily offended. They are like the people Jesus referred to in the Gospels who hear the Word, accept it, and bear fruit—some 30 percent, some 60 percent, and some 100 percent! (See Matt. 13:23; Mark 4:8, 20.) The people in these verses obtained results because they received the Word into "good ground"—into a good and honest heart.

Let's look again at the Word that didn't bear fruit, because it was planted in a "stony" heart.

MARK 4:16–17

16 And these are they likewise which are sown on stony ground; who, when they have heard the word, immediately receive it with gladness;

17 And have no root in themselves, and so endure but for a time: afterward, when affliction or persecution ariseth for the word's sake, immediately they are offended.

This person receives the Word gladly, but it goes on to say that he doesn't endure till the end, but only "for a time."

Why? Because something happened to cause him to *stop* enduring, or to give up and quit. What was it? Tribulation or persecution. In other words, at the first sign of trouble, this person became offended; he *stumbled.*

The *Bible in Basic English* says, *". . . they quickly become full of doubts."*

The *English Standard Version* says, *". . . immediately they fall away."*

The *Good News Translation* says, *". . . they give up at once."*

Offense will steal from you your spiritual stability— your ability to endure in tough times. Offense will cause you to stumble—to doubt, fall away, and quit!

Understanding Enemy Strategy

I made reference to this previously, but if I could drive home one truth in the heart of every believer, it would be the truth that *offense is Satan's strategy to get him out of the will of God and rob him of God's intended best.* If the enemy can't discourage a believer and get him to give up on his faith, he will distract him some other way, and often that "other way" is through offense.

The good news is, someone else's wrong actions cannot keep you out of the will of God. But if *you* react wrongly, your own wrong actions can cause you to miss God's highest and best for your life. That is tremendous food for thought!

Let us dare allow ourselves to consider the possibility that we can avoid so much trouble by simply choosing rightly and refusing to take offense.

Chapter 4

How to Tell If You Are Trapped by Offense

In this chapter we're going to look at telltale signs we've been trapped by offense so that we can extract ourselves from its venomous snare.

Sign Number One: You're Offended Because of *Someone Else's* Offense

Recently, God dealt with me about this aspect of harboring offense. He said to me, "Many of My people who know the Word are not living where I want them to live, because of offense." Then He said something else that astounded me. He said, "And many times, it's not even their offense. They have picked up someone else's offense."

As I said before, some people are unaware that offense is stirring within them. They'll say, "I have a great family, a great job, great friends, and I attend a great church. Everything is fantastic. Why should I be offended?" Yet every time they hear a certain person's name mentioned, they become upset or angry because of what the person supposedly did to hurt someone they care about.

Fanning the Flames of Offense

We know offense can occur a number of ways, and one of those ways is through *insults*. In other words, if someone were to attack you verbally, you would probably become offended. Offenses also come when there's *strife, division,* and *backbiting.* But notice the culprit in each of these causes of offense: *the tongue!*

Let's look at a familiar passage in James concerning the power of the tongue.

JAMES 3:2–5 (NLT)

2 We all make many mistakes, but those who control their tongues can also control themselves in every other way.

3 We can make a large horse turn around and go wherever we want by means of a small bit in its mouth.

4 And a tiny rudder makes a huge ship turn wherever the pilot wants it to go, even though the winds are strong.

5 So also, the tongue is a small thing, but WHAT ENORMOUS DAMAGE IT CAN DO. A tiny spark can set a great forest on fire.

Have you ever witnessed someone's words causing a great "fire" to occur? And have you ever seen that fire *spread* because of words?

When an offense occurs, it often spreads like wildfire when the person who was offended begins repeating the offense to others. Why? Because he wants others to become offended too! And it often works: People will become offended because of what someone else did to their spouse, relative, friend, or co-worker. They weren't involved in the situation at all, but they become offended nevertheless.

How does this happen? Let's suppose someone you know gets hurt by another person, and this friend or loved one confides in you about it, repeating in great detail the entire incident start to finish. If you're not careful, those words can begin to affect the way you view your loved one's offender, especially if the person who's been wounded talks about it over and over again, day after day. If you keep listening to this person's grievance, before long, offense will begin to stir in you over something you never even experienced!

We need to be cautious when someone begins talking to us about someone else. Sometimes people legitimately want to work past their offense, and they need to confide in someone to help them work through the process God's way. But sometimes, the only reason people want to tell someone else about their trouble is to stir that other person up too—to fan the flames of offense!

A person who likes to spread offense to others could be characterized as a *talebearer*. More often than not, a talebearer will portray himself in the best possible light when telling his side of the story. And he will portray the other person in the worst possible light. Why? To gain pity or sympathy so that we will side with him against that other person!

We need to guard ourselves against taking up someone else's offense. No matter who's been wounded or how much we love him or her, if we become offended, too, we may pay a great price for what we think is simply lending a sympathetic ear!

In other words, we might think we're helping and being a good friend by listening to the repeated complaints of someone who's been hurt. But if we take on the offense ourselves, we could find ourselves in a position spiritually where we can no longer help anyone.

Sign Number Two:
You Resent Someone Else's Blessing

Another sign you may be trapped by offense is if you resent the fact that someone received a blessing.

We need to be careful that when someone else is blessed, we maintain our attitude of faith. If we don't, we may fall through that trap door of offense! The Bible says that God is no respecter of persons (Acts 10:34). What He has done for anyone else, He will do for us too. So if we're upset because someone else got blessed, we might need to check up on our faith. If we really believe we're in line for the same blessing, we will rejoice with that other person and maintain an attitude of joyful expectation about what we're believing God for!

I have also seen people become offended when someone else got blessed—not because of the person's blessing, per se, but because the person used his faith to receive it! Those who became offended knew they had slacked off and weren't using their faith as they should. They weren't believing God to meet their needs and desires, and they became upset when someone else believed God and received from Him!

Sign Number Three: You Continually Speak Negatively About Someone

Still another telltale sign you may be harboring offense is if you are continually speaking negatively about someone. If every time a person's name is mentioned, you say something negative about him or bring up some negative experience in connection with him, you have probably been caught in offense's sinister trap. You need to recognize it and release that person immediately, refusing to allow any ill will or animosity in your heart toward that individual.

Sign Number Four: You 'Rejoice' at Someone's Misfortune

Another sign you've been snared by offense is if you become happy or excited when something bad happens to someone who has offended you.

As I said before, people don't usually want to admit it if they're offended and don't want to see another person blessed. They are probably painfully aware that they're supposed to love others and care about what happens to them. And they probably know all too well that the love of God has been shed abroad in the heart of every believer (Rom. 5:5). But perhaps they don't realize that the subtle workings of offense will "choke" that love and keep it from manifesting outwardly toward others. They need to acknowledge their offense, ask God to forgive them, and then forgive the person who offended them.

Sign Number Five: You Habitually Fellowship With Offended People!

Another sign you may have fallen into offense's trap is if you're running with a crowd of offended people!

In my 50 years of ministry, I have observed that when people become offended, they often surround themselves with as many people as possible who will take up their offense. *They want others to be offended at their offender!*

I have also noticed that offended people often run in groups. In other words, they attract one another in friend-ships because they draw to themselves others who are harboring grudges and negative emotions toward other people. That way, they'll always have someone to complain to who will "understand" them and sympathize with them because of what they're going through.

As these offended people get together, they often take their negative emotions with them into other situations, and they can split churches, prayer groups, and other relationships. They can cause disharmony among friends, married couples, or co-workers on the job. Because they never dealt with their offense, they seem to go through life *expecting* to be offended, and they often come across to others as hostile and antagonistic.

You might say, "Well, I know So-and-so has a chip on his shoulder. He's mad at the world. But I can still hang around him. I can influence him for good; I won't take on his negativity."

Friend, that attitude is not scriptural. The Bible has something to say about the company we keep and the effect it will have on our lives.

1 CORINTHIANS 15:33 (NIV)

33 Do not be misled: "Bad company corrupts good character."

PROVERBS 13:20 (NIV)

20 He who walks with the wise grows wise, but a companion of fools suffers harm.

Please don't misunderstand me. I'm not saying you shouldn't try to help people who have erred from the path, so to speak. And certainly you should walk in love toward an individual who is carrying a grudge and needs to see the love of God in demonstration. But that doesn't mean you have to become a close friend to that kind of person.

The environment you live in will influence what you eventually become! You *will* be affected by your associations and your environment—for good or for evil. If you live in a negative atmosphere, you will eventually become a negative person. On the other hand, if you live in a positive environment, you will become increasingly positive in your attitudes.

When I was in the eighth grade, my teacher asked each student to bring a five-pound bag of potatoes to school for an experiment. We were instructed to empty our bags. Then she gave each student a rotten potato to place at the bottom of his or her bag. Then we refilled our bags with the potatoes we brought from home.

Each bag was labeled with our names and placed high on a shelf for days. The next time we checked our bags, several of the potatoes close to the rotten potato at the bottom of the bag were showing signs of decay. Days later, more potatoes were affected. Before long, the entire bag had decayed. All the potatoes had been "infected" by the one rotten potato.

Likewise, if you keep company with a "rotten potato"—someone who has allowed himself to become infected with bitterness and negativity over an offense—you are going to be affected. Over time, their "rotten" attitude toward life will influence your way of thinking, believing, and acting. You will eventually take up their offense—and you'll probably do it without even realizing what happened.

Forgiveness—The Prevention and the Cure

When someone wrongs you, it can be a challenge to forgive him. But if the person wrongs you *repeatedly,* the challenge will feel insurmountable. In fact, you will probably not feel like forgiving him at all!

"But these feelings of unforgiveness are so strong," someone might argue. Yet the strongest feelings cannot override your determined decision to do what's right. You may have to reaffirm several times that you've forgiven the person who wronged you. But eventually, your feelings will change.

Many people are waiting for their feelings to change before they'll forgive. But it doesn't work that way. You need to make a quality decision to forgive right in the face of negative feelings. Then and only then will those feelings come in line with your decision.

The disciples also dealt with the temptation to harbor unforgiveness. Let's look at how Jesus instructed them. (This applies to us today.)

LUKE 17:4 (NKJV)

4 "And if he sins against you seven times in a day, and seven times in a day returns to you, saying, 'I repent,' you shall forgive him."

Notice Jesus said, "You *shall* forgive him." That means that forgiveness is a command, not a suggestion or an option!

Why was Jesus being so adamant about the issue of forgiveness? Because unforgiveness will ensnare you and hinder you spiritually, keeping you from fulfilling and receiving God's highest and best in life. And forgiveness will not only keep you from becoming ensnared, it will also free you from the clutches of offense if you've missed it and sinned by harboring an offense. Forgiveness acts as a prevention *and* a cure!

Forgiveness in Marriage

Learning to forgive will also help you in your marriage. So often you hear married people say, "I just don't love her anymore," or, "I just don't love him anymore." Those people haven't learned the truth that they can control their feelings simply by making the right choices!

We looked at the power of the tongue to cause offense and even to spread offense. And we looked at forgiveness as the key to escaping the dark prison of offense. But did you know that words can imprison you or set you free? In other words, if offense has adversely affected your relationship with your spouse, your tongue probably got you into the mess you're in—and your tongue can get you out!

If you as a husband or wife will make a quality decision to love your spouse and then begin talking about how much you love and value your mate, your feelings toward that person will change. Things may not change overnight, but just as the small rudder of a ship can change the course of the whole ship, your tongue can change the course of your life!

Choose Life!

As a believer, how you respond to offense will determine the success of your future. How far you go in life will be determined by what you do with each opportunity to become offended.

Some people are always wondering and even fretting about the future. They haven't realized that they have more to say about their success or failure in life than anyone else, including God! In Deuteronomy 30:19, the Lord says, *"I call heaven and earth to record this day against you, that I have set before you life and death, blessing and cursing: THEREFORE CHOOSE LIFE, that both thou and thy seed may live."*

Offenses *will* come your way in life, but you must recognize when you are actually in the trap of offense and quickly deal with it. We will look at some ways to escape Satan's snare in the next chapter.

Chapter 5

Escaping Satan's Snare

Previously we have touched on the fact that Satan uses offense as a strategy to distract and deter the believer from doing God's will and receiving His highest and best in life. But the sum total of the enemy's goal is not simply to distract a believer from God's best; rather, it is to completely entrap and destroy that believer!

Anytime you become offended and harbor ill will toward someone, your spiritual growth is halted and you cease to move forward and make progress from that point. In other words, you become "stuck" in the dark wasteland of offense.

People who become offended and fail to deal with it get stuck on their offense and can't move forward in life.

For example, have you ever crossed paths with someone you haven't seen for awhile—and just minutes into your conversation, he brings up some offense of the past? The offense may have occurred months or even years ago, yet he talks about it as if it happened yesterday! This person got "stuck" in life and failed to make progress from the point in time that he succumbed to offense.

Have you ever gotten your car stuck in mud or snow? After attempting to maneuver the vehicle every way you possibly could, you realized that unless something changed, you weren't going anywhere. You would either have to wait for someone to tow the car—or wait for the mud to dry or the snow to melt!

Similarly, if you've been "stuck" in one position because of offense, you can free yourself from that entrapment and begin making spiritual progress once again.

We said in Chapter One that one definition of offense is *to entrap or impede*. Satan doesn't just want to impede or hinder your progress—he wants to *stop you altogether*! And if you'll allow him to do it, he will capture you in his trap of offense, where he will try to destroy you.

Have you ever found yourself bound in some area of your life? You were walking with God and running your race, but slowly—over time—you began to get off track? Or maybe you were minding your own business when, *bam,* out of nowhere, someone hurt you. Perhaps it was a business partner who cheated you out of money, a friend who rejected you, or a spouse who betrayed you. You thought you were making progress spiritually, but then your life came to a standstill.

I will share with you an example that loosely illustrates this scenario in the natural. I ran track in high school, and during one particular race, I still had plenty of kick left, but two runners from the same team were running directly in front of me. At the same time I tried to go around them, another guy came running up beside me. There was no room for me to go forward or around without fouling someone. I was completely hemmed in, but I remained in the race.

In life, a person could feel so hemmed in, overwhelmed by his pain and misfortune, that he allows himself to be permanently removed from his spiritual race. He becomes immobilized through offense, trapped in his own prison of bitterness.

Caught in the Trap of Offense

Sadly, today we hear of so many bound by things such as drugs and alcohol. Their indulgences of the past have ensnared them in a prison of their own making. Yet how many people are bound by offense? *Plenty!* They indulge their flesh by allowing their mind to dwell on what someone else did to them; and they cling to all the negative emotions that come with being offended. Because they continually meditate on the offense, they are swept away into a prison of bitterness.

You may feel as if you're in prison today because of offense. But I want to encourage you; there is hope for the person ensnared by offense just as there is hope for someone who's been ensnared by drugs, alcohol, or by some other addiction. Just don't throw away the key! Don't refuse to repent, forgive, and renew your mind with the Word of God concerning God's love and forgiveness.

Another definition of offense paints a picture of the trigger or moveable stick that opens wide a trap door. In other words, offense can take hold in your mind to such a degree that it's as if the ground beneath you suddenly gives way, plunging you into deep darkness!

I once heard about people in other countries using certain bait and maneuvers to capture monkeys without harming them. They would drill a hole into a coconut, empty the milk, and place a shiny pebble inside the shell. Then they would chain the coconut shell to a tree and wait. Out of natural curiosity, the monkey will approach the coconut and reach its hand into the hole to retrieve the pebble. The monkey grasps the shiny object, but since the hole isn't big enough to accommodate the monkey's fist, the animal is trapped! Unless it releases the pebble, it is unable to escape the coconut trap. Most of the monkeys keep a tight grip on the pebble and refuse to let go, not realizing how vulnerable they've made themselves to being captured.

Notice that as long as the monkey keeps its hand outstretched, it is free to move its hand in and out of that coconut shell as it pleases. But when the monkey becomes possessive of the shiny pebble, it finds itself hopelessly trapped. You could say that monkey is trapped in a prison of its own making!

Caught in a Trap

So many people are caught in a "monkey trap" because they refuse to let go of offense. At first, their flesh enjoyed meditating on how someone had hurt them. But then they became ensnared—trapped—by their desire to be angry, bitter, and unforgiving.

It's time for us as believers to wake up and realize that Satan has laid a "minefield" of offenses before us, and he is just waiting for us to be destroyed by it. But God has made a way for us to live free from the trap offense.

The Three Rs of Protecting Yourself Against Offense

You can't keep people from offending you, but you *can* guard yourself against taking offense and harboring offense when a wrong has been committed—or even when you *perceive* that a wrong has been committed.

There are three keys to protecting yourself against this deadly enemy called offense: (1) *realize* that offenses *will* come; (2) *recognize* offense for what it is—a spiritual enemy; and (3) *refuse* to allow offense to take root in your heart or mind.

The First R: *Realize*

Most of us have heard the saying that there are two things on earth that are inevitable: death and taxes! But the Bible talks about something else as being inevitable—it says, "Offenses *will* come."

LUKE 17:1

1 Then said he [Jesus] unto the disciples, IT IS IMPOSSIBLE BUT THAT OFFENCES WILL COME: but woe unto him, through whom they come!

Other translations of this verse read as follows:

". . . *Occasions for stumbling are bound to come. . .* " (New Revised Standard Version)

". . . *It's impossible for the stumbling blocks not to come. . .* " (Young's Literal Translation)

". . . *It is inevitable that causes of stumbling should come. . .* " (Weymouth New Testament)

". . . *It is inevitable that there should be snares. . .* " (Twentieth Century New Testament)

". . . *It is inevitable that stumbling blocks should come. . .* " (New American Standard Bible)

Notice the two different words for offense listed here: *stumbling blocks* and *snares*. Stumbling blocks and snares *will* come, but realizing this fact helps us prepare and protect ourselves against them when they do.

The Inevitability of Offense

Someday, somewhere, someone is going to say or do something that will offend you. Maybe the offender will be someone who is habitually insensitive or discourteous, or perhaps the person will unknowingly touch on a "nerve" concerning something that is an issue with you.

We need to realize that offenses *will* come our way—it is inevitable. But whether or not we will become entrapped and ensnared by them is a choice we get to make!

The Second R: *Recognize*

Some people have trouble identifying offense, either because they don't want to identify it or because they simply don't recognize what they're feeling as offense. If you can't recognize offense, it is difficult to guard against it.

For example, have you ever heard someone say, "When So-and-so said that to me, I felt insulted and attacked"? Yet that person was hesitant to say, "I was offended by what he said," or, "That offended me."

Or someone might say, "That is the most discourteous person I've ever met." The one making that observation might think he is doing just that: simply making an observation. Yet he is more likely offended by the other person's discourteous behavior, whether he will admit it or not.

So you see, offense *will* come. Even if what someone said seems trivial in retrospect, if you were offended, you need to make a conscious effort to release any and all ill-will and ill-feeling toward the offender. You may think it's not important, but it is *very* important to recognize offense as it comes in its various forms and to take steps to deal with it according to God's Word.

Certainly, there are times when someone's offense is so great that those who are hurt by his or her actions are immediately offended. That kind of offense is easy to recognize. But how often do we allow offense into our lives more slowly and subtly? As days and weeks pass, what began as some seemingly small matter festers and swells, and we become more and more at odds with the person we're offended by. After a time, those feelings of unpleasantness that we feel toward him or her begin to harass us constantly.

When we first begin having those feelings, we might not recognize the fact that we're offended. However, as time passes, the reality is that we have let the actions of another affect us in such a way that we are now harboring offense.

The Third R: *Refuse*

Someone asked, "Since offenses *will* come, how can we keep from being offended?"

You can keep offense from gaining an entrance into your heart in much the same you might refuse to open the front door to your home every time someone knocks. In other words, just because someone is knocking at your door doesn't mean you have to open it and let the person in. What if you don't recognize the person at your door—and you're home alone? There's no rule or law that requires you to open your door just based on someone knocking!

Similarly, just because offense comes knocking at your door doesn't mean you have to let it in! You can refuse to give place to offense; you can turn around and walk away.

On the other hand, you could open the door to offense, entertain it, and allow it to take up residence in your heart. The choice is yours whether you will *take* offense or *refuse* offense. When you're faced with the decision of whether you'll harbor an offense, consider this: It is just as easy to pray for that other person, "Lord, forgive him," as it is to meditate on whatever the person said or did to offend you. But if you hesitate to forgive and refuse the offense, it will begin closing its vice-like grip on your life.

Have you ever heard the saying, "Just let it roll off you like water off of a duck's back"? When a duck dives underwater, the feathers closest to its body remain dry. If you look closely enough, you can see beads of water on its outer feathers, but the water just "rolls off." The reason is, a duck's feathers are coated with a certain kind of oil that repels water and wetness. That oil won't allow the feathers to become saturated.

Similarly, when we feel overwhelmed by offense, we have the ability to remain "dry" and unaffected by the offense because of the oil of the Holy Spirit in our lives! Because of the love of God that has been shed abroad in our hearts by the Holy Ghost, we can let offense roll off of us like water off of a duck's back!

'Teflon' Christianity

Most people in this country own some type of cookware that's covered with a nonstick coating. One particular brand name for this kind of coating is Teflon. Teflon coating is advertised to keep food from sticking to the pan as you cook and make cleaning the pan easier.

Similarly, God has designed a "nonstick coating" for your life, and it's called *forgiveness*! When you learn how to walk in love and forgiveness, offenses—though they will come—will not be able to stick to you and corrode, corrupt, or harm you in any way.

With a nonstick pan, even if some food does remain in the pan, just one swish of a cloth or paper towel removes it and leaves the pan's surface shiny and clean. In much the same way, even if offense tries to attach itself to you, with just one application of prayer, you can wipe the slate clean, so to speak, and go on with your life as if you were never offended in the first place.

John L. Mason, renowned motivational speaker and author, said, "When you've been wronged, a poor memory is the best response."[1] That's a simple but profound statement. Refusing offense is still the best policy!

Offense will come to us in many ways. We must *realize* that fact, learn to *recognize* offense when it comes, and *refuse* to allow it to attach itself to our lives.

---

[1] John L. Mason, *You Were Born an Original, Don't Die a Copy* (Tulsa: Insight International, 1993), 67.

Chapter 6

A Good Defense Against Offense

We all must continually guard our heart against offense. No one is exempt from the temptation to become offended and harbor grudges and other negative emotions. One of our first lines of defense against offense is simply to realize that offenses *will* come; opportunities to succumb to offense will present themselves to *everyone* at one time or another.

Since we understand that offenses will come, we need to ask ourselves, *Do we have a good defense in place to keep the enemy from gaining the victory over our lives?*

In any competitive sport, if you truly want to win, you're going to have to have a good defense. You could have a great offense, but if your defense is deficient, you're not going to win very many games.

Similarly, if you're going to win in life, you need a good defense against Satan's offense.

Offenses come from Satan. Offense is his strategy to keep you from fulfilling God's will and to ultimately destroy you. We have thought that offenses came from people—from our jealous co-worker, a shady business-man, or even our spouse or close friend. But the Bible says, *". . . we wrestle not against flesh and blood, but against principalities, against powers, against the rulers of the darkness of this world, against spiritual wickedness in high places"* (Eph. 6:12).

For too long, we have made people—flesh and blood— the enemy. But people are not the enemy; *Satan* is the enemy. Certainly, people can yield to Satan and cause problems, but the root of our problems in life is the devil, not people.

Failure in a Christian's life can often be attributed to one of two causes: (1) The person didn't understand who his enemy was; and (2) he didn't understand how his enemy operates.

In any successful military campaign—and certainly in any sports competition—you first have to know who your enemy is! Second, you must know how the opposition operates. Studying the enemy's past strategies and maneuvers will put you in a more favorable position to win.

We already know that Satan uses offense to come against us and defeat us. But what happens when we recognize his strategy and cut him off at the pass by refusing offense when others wrong us in some way? He will come against us *another* way!

In the game of football, the goal is to run the ball into the opponent's end zone in order to score. If we're running with the ball, spiritually speaking, and Satan can't tackle us or trip us up with some blatant offense, he will rely on his backup—another linebacker, a safety, or a defensive back, so to speak—to try to take us down before we gain another victory.

Let's bring that illustration home spiritually. If Satan can't distract you from the blessings of God through someone who offends you, he will begin to look elsewhere to steal from you and to destroy you if possible.

For example, as we saw in the last chapter, the devil may send someone across your path that is offended. In telling you his or her story, you become indignant and even outraged because of the magnitude of the injustice that was perpetrated against this person. Before you know it, you have picked up this person's offense! You recognized the enemy's strategy when he influenced someone to offend you personally, and you forgave that person. But you fell for Satan's second line of defense, and now you're hopping mad because *someone else* got hurt!

Satan is clever enough to have a backup plan against us. We should be spiritually smart enough to have a solid, successive line of defense against him!

Building Your Defense

One of the first things a coach has to take into consideration when putting a team together is how he's going to build a good defense.

What kind of "player" is necessary to resist the offense when it comes? In other words, what are the characteristics of an outstanding defensive player that is skilled at taking down the opponent's offensive moves?

Number One:
He Continually Abides in the Word

We've already read Psalm 119:165, but now let's look at this verse in the New King James Version.

PSALMS 119:165 (NKJV)

165 Great peace have those who love Your law, And nothing causes them to stumble.

The Law in David's time was the Law of God as written in the Pentateuch, or what we know as the first five Books of the Bible. So this verse is talking about loving God's Word. When you love God's Word, nothing can make you stumble and fall away from it—*nothing!*

PSALM 119:11,105 (NKJV)

11 Your word I have hidden in my heart, That I might not sin against You!

105 Your word is a lamp to my feet And a light to my path....

The Word of God is light to our path. With the Word of God in our heart, we can see where we're going so that we won't stumble. Another verse in Psalms says, *"For with You is the fountain of life; In Your light we see light"* (Ps. 36:9 NKJV). As we keep a firm hold on the Word of God in our heart, not only can we see where we're going, we can recognize offense when it comes.

Offense comes to steal the Word from our heart, but if we will be diligent to guard our heart and to keep it solidly planted within, that Word will bring forth fruit, and there's nothing the enemy or anyone else can do about it!

Number Two: He Exhibits the Fruit of the Spirit

Developing the fruit of the Spirit in your life will empower you so that you have a defense against Satan's offense.

GALATIANS 5:22–23

22 But the fruit of the Spirit is love, joy, peace, longsuffering, gentleness, goodness, faith,

23 Meekness, temperance: against such there is no law.

The last phrase in this passage says, *". . . against such* [against the fruit of the Spirit] *there is no law."* When you're walking in the fruit of the Spirit, you're manifesting fruits of righteousness, or the characteristics of God. And you will not be easily swayed when the temptation to sin comes your way. Another way to say it is like this: When God *in* you is in control of your life, Satan cannot gain control!

You would have to relinquish your position for Satan to get a foothold in your life and make you stumble.

As I said before, my father was known as a man who walked in the God-kind of love as much as he walked in the God-kind of faith. He was highly developed in the fruit of the Spirit. People often commented about Dad that he was longsuffering, saying, "Nothing ever upsets that man."

Dad had such a tremendous love for God's Word and for the things of God. Every time Dad received more light on a subject, he was quick to walk in that light. That's why he never stumbled due to offense.

Number Three:
He Chooses His Teammates Wisely

So far, we've looked at two characteristics of the person who has built a good defense against Satan's offense: (1) he continually abides in the Word; (2) he exhibits the fruit of the Spirit.

Now let's look at the third characteristic of a skillful "defensive player": *He chooses his teammates wisely.*

Previously, we looked at the verses, *"Do not be misled: 'Bad company corrupts good character'"* (1 Cor. 15:33

NIV) and, *"He who walks with the wise grows wise, but a companion of fools suffers harm"* (Prov. 13:20 NIV).

These are just two of the many verses we could cite that talk about this subject directly or give instances in which a person's poorly chosen friendships hindered him in his spiritual walk and his obedience to God. The Bible is plain: The company we keep will influence us for good or for evil. We can question that or second-guess it until "Kingdom come," but it's true anyway! God's Word is eternally, irrefutably true, and since He says that the company we keep will influence us, then *the company we keep will influence us!* It's just that simple!

Have you ever noticed that people tend to become like those they socialize with or hang out with on a regular basis? It may not happen in a day, a week, or a month, but over time, we become like those we associate with. That's why most of us as young people were admonished by our parents, teachers, or caregivers, "Choose your friends wisely!"

Now, when I talk about being influenced by someone you associate with, I'm talking about taking on certain aspects of his character and even some of his opinions and viewpoints. That's fine if that other person loves God and bases his entire life and way of living on God's Word. But it's not fine at all if that person is rebellious and worldly in this thinking—even if he calls himself a Christian!

Let's suppose for a moment that you make a new friend with whom you enjoy spending time. But after a period of time, you begin noticing that he has a bitter attitude toward ministers, for example, or that he doesn't like certain groups or denominations and never has anything nice to say about them.

You notice that your new "friend" is critical toward others and seems offended at numerous people. You try to overlook all of these things because of the common interests you share with your friend. You even reason that you could have a positive influence on this person. So you remain in close fellowship with him or her.

However, over time—little by little—you begin thinking the same bitter thoughts you've heard your "friend" talk about time and time again. You develop an intolerant, critical attitude toward other believers who don't believe just like you do. Because of this new friendship, you become tempted to reclaim as your enemies the people you forgave in the past. Your thought-life is continually negative. And to top it all off, when someone points all this out to you in meekness and love, you become hostile and offended at him!

What's worse, you feel devoid of faith, and the things you were praying about either become unimportant, or you begin forfeiting answers to prayer because you've lost your spiritual footing and your ability to endure.

Why did all these things happen? You failed to choose your "teammates" wisely, and that "bad company" you insisted on keeping corrupted you in your mind, your emotions, and your actions.

Satan has crept into many churches because of people's failure to choose their associations wisely. For example, in selecting people to work within a team setting, such as the volunteer staff at your church, it's important to keep offense out, or the enemy could wreak havoc throughout the entire church.

Some people become offended when they're not selected for a position for which they volunteered in the church. For example, maybe they signed up to become a choir member, but they can't carry a tune! The choir director or music minister gently encourages them to volunteer in another capacity or in another area of the church, and they become angry and offended.

A person has to have more than a *desire* to serve in certain areas of the ministry; he must also *be qualified*. And if he isn't qualified, instead of becoming offended, he needs to get quiet before God about where he should serve.

A corporation can't afford to fill positions with people who aren't qualified to handle the demands of those positions. To do so would not only affect morale within the organization, it could spell financial disaster for the entire company. Why do people think church leadership would want to run a church with any less degree of excellence and professionalism?

Some people become offended when they are passed over for a promotion or raise they thought they deserved. I realize that people can make mistakes and that deserving people can genuinely be overlooked and slighted on the job. But offense is not the way to handle the situation! In fact, becoming offended is a sure sign they aren't supposed to be in those positions. People who become offended and start telling everyone they see about it are almost certain never to be placed in leadership, because talebearers don't make good team players or good leaders.

As a pastor, I have noticed that people who begin attending a new church because they became offended at their old church will eventually become offended at the new church! If you were to examine their history, they probably have a pattern of moving from church to church to church. They never settled anywhere and became faithful, useful members of a local congregation.

Christians who are solidly grounded in the Word will not be up one day when the circumstances are favorable and down the next day when they're not. They won't be loving their brother one day and cussing him out the next!

I've seen people behave this way with churches, with jobs, and with relationships. Their lives are a picture of instability. They can't stay put and stand their ground, because they're always getting offended at something or someone. Everywhere they go, they encounter the same problems— because they never dealt with the issue of offense in their life. And the cycle will never end until they see the light and decide to put a stop to it, saying, *"No more!"*

Not only is it important to choose your teammates wisely, it's important to *be* the right kind of teammate. There's not one of us that doesn't have to take ourselves by the collar, so to speak, and give ourselves a pep talk every once in awhile about how we are or are not going to behave. If we really want to, we can tell ourselves to straighten up as well as anyone else can!

Number Four: He Keeps a Clear Conscience

The fourth characteristic of a skillful "defensive player": *He keeps a clear conscience.*

ACTS 24:16 (NKJV)

16 Paul said, "This being so [talking about the resurrection of the dead], I myself always strive to have a conscience without offense toward God and men."

ACTS 24:16 (NIV)

16 "So I [Paul] strive always to keep my conscience clear before God and man."

ACTS 24:16 (Amplified)

16 Therefore I always exercise and discipline myself [mortifying my body, deadening my carnal affections, bodily appetites, and worldly desires, endeavoring in all respects] to have a clear (unshaken, blameless) conscience, void of offense toward God and toward men.

Because of Paul's belief in the coming resurrection, he said he endeavored to keep his conscience clear before God and man. Paul diligently kept his flesh under the control of his spirit by disciplining himself in spiritual things.

Like Paul, we can develop ourselves to instantly recognize and avoid things that cause us to sin and grieve the heart of God. We can get to the place where we will hear something ungodly, such as gossip or slander, and an "alarm" will go off in our spirit warning us not to listen.

Many aircrafts are equipped with navigation systems that will automatically alert the pilot if the craft is flying too close to another object. Some planes contain devices that will broadcast the recording, "Pull up! Pull up!" if the pilot flies within a dangerous range of one of these objects. When the plane is landing, this type of system will also broadcast periodic air-to-ground distances for the duration of the plane's descent. Even when the plane is too high for the pilot to see where he is landing, he knows exactly where he is in relation to the ground.

In much the same way, when you've trained yourself in the Word to be spiritually sensitive, your spirit will start talking to you if you get too close to sinning or missing the mark! The voice of your conscience will alert you, giving you a warning signal that danger lies ahead. If someone says something you shouldn't listen to, your conscience will know it and will caution you. Even if you start to say something you shouldn't say, that voice will witness to you that you should keep quiet instead.

In review, the person who successfully builds a good defense against the offense that will invariably come his way does the following things consistently:

1. He continually abides in the Word.

2. He exhibits the fruit of the Spirit.

3. He chooses his teammates wisely.

4. He keeps a clear conscience.

The enemy knows that as long as you stay with the Word, you will be fruitful, you will bring glory to God, and he won't be able to touch you! So what do you think his "game plan" is for distracting you from the goal set before you: to choke the Word of God in your heart so that it is no longer effective! Perhaps Satan has a play in his playbook called "Operation Offense." I don't know, but I do know that offense is one of his evil strategies aimed against God's creation, man—and especially against those who have been recreated by God in Christ Jesus.

We must keep a firm grip on the Word at all times if we're going to succeed in life. And we must realize that every day, we will have opportunities to decide whether we will go with the Word or with opposing circumstances. If we side with the circumstances of life, we will be overthrown in our faith. But if we side with the Word, we will be upheld in our faith, and our faith will not fail us!

James 4:7 says, *"Submit yourselves therefore to God. Resist the devil, and he will flee from you."* When we yield to offense, we are yielding to the devil's influence, and we certainly don't have *him* on the run. Instead, he has *us* on the run.

But if we build a good defense, resisting and refusing his offense, we are yielding ourselves to God's influence. And the Bible says that when we do that, we will put the devil on the run every time!

Chapter 7

Love Triumphs Over Offense

One might argue that the prevalence of offense—unfor-giveness, bitterness, and hatred—is a sign of the times we are living in. I want to look at a passage in Second Timothy concerning the last days.

2 TIMOTHY 3:1–5 (NIV)

1 But mark this: There will be terrible times in the last days.

2 People will be lovers of themselves, lovers of money, boastful, proud, abusive, disobedient to their parents, ungrateful, unholy,

3 without love, unforgiving, slanderous, without self-control, brutal, not lovers of the good,

4 treacherous, rash, conceited, lovers of pleasure rather than lovers of God—

5 having a form of godliness but denying its power. Have nothing to do with them.

With all the ways we could be offended and all the reasons we could harbor unforgiveness in our heart today, there is a refreshing, timeless truth that surpasses the sin and darkness of the world around us, and that is the truth that *love triumphs over offense.*

1 CORINTHIANS 13:4–8 (Amplified)

4 Love endures long and is patient and kind; love never is envious nor boils over with jealousy, is not boastful or vainglorious, does not display itself haughtily.

5 It is not conceited (arrogant and inflated with pride); it is not rude (unmannerly) and does not act unbecomingly. Love (God's love in us) does not insist on its own rights or its own way, for it is not self-seeking; it is not touchy or fretful or resentful; it takes no account of the evil done to it [it pays no attention to a suffered wrong].

6 It does not rejoice at injustice and unrighteousness, but rejoices when right and truth prevail.

7 Love bears up under anything and everything that comes, is ever ready to believe the best of every person, its hopes are fadeless under all circumstances, and it endures everything [without weakening].

8 Love never fails [never fades out or becomes obsolete or comes to an end]. . . .

Here we see a description of God's love and of the kind of love we're to show toward others. Notice it doesn't say, for example, "Love endures long and is patient and kind— *as long as no one gives me a hard time."* No, these verses in First Corinthians 13 apply to us no matter what anyone else has done to us.

Have you ever noticed in reading these scriptures that love never gives an offense or receives an offense? I realize that we all miss it from time to time and say or do something unkind that we shouldn't have said or done. Or we may inadvertently offend someone. But we are to continually grow in love and make walking in love our great aim and quest.

I grew up in a home where I saw the God-kind of love modeled by my father. As a pastor and then an itinerate minister, he suffered all kinds of injustices and mistreatment by others. But he made it his practice to walk in love and to refuse offense no matter what. And he would often say to me, "Son, always take the high road in life. Anybody can wallow in the mud down on the low road."

Love Will Cause You to Rise Above Offense

The God-kind of love, or God's love in you, will buoy you up, strengthen you, and help you rise above the offenses that come your way. If you will walk in this kind of love consistently, you will not harbor offense when it comes.

Allowing God's love to operate in us will also cause us to rise to a higher level spiritually. Walking in the God-kind of love consistently will enable us to let go of the attitudes and habits of the past, and help us to rise to a level of living that we have yet to experience.

Let's look at some characteristics of God's love in First Corinthians 13:4–8 that will keep us on the "high road," high above the troubling "low road" of bitterness, unforgiveness, and offense.

Love Is Patient and Kind

Verse 4 in *The Amplified Bible* says, *"Love endures long and is patient and kind."* Most of us don't like those words "endure" and "long," because they imply we will have to put up with something that we really don't want to have to deal with!

We don't particularly like to hear messages about patience, either, because we are a fast-paced, *now* generation, and we like the fact that, especially in this country, we can have instant gratification for almost any need. For example, we have instant breakfasts when we're on the go, 10-minute lunches when we're crunching time, drive-through restaurants, dry cleaners, and banks to save us even more time, and even instant credit when we don't want to wait to buy something that we really want.

However, when it comes to dealing with others, we need to learn patience. *We need to be patient with people!*

I don't know a single person on this planet who is perfect—who has matured completely and reached full perfection. We're supposed to be maturing in Christ daily as we walk with Him, but no one has "arrived"—every believer has room to grow in his or her Christian walk.

Every one of us could wear a sign around our neck that reads "Under Construction," and we'd be telling the truth about it! We're all at various stages of building. Some are even rebuilding due to a spiritual or moral collapse because their foundation wasn't grounded in Christ. We need to be patient with one another and see each other for what we can become in Christ, not just for what we appear to be today.

Love endures long and is patient. Love is also *kind.* To be kind means to be *gentle* or *mild-mannered.* Have you ever known someone who just has to have the last word in a disagreement, even when he or she knows that continuing to speak will only make matters worse? Showing kindness can sometimes mean backing down from an argument.

Being kind also means not snapping back at someone who's being unfriendly, perhaps because he or she is having a really bad day. Many times, I've heard people say, "I'm going to give So-and-so a piece of my mind!" Often I've thought to myself as I've heard that, *Better hold on to your piece of mind. If you give away too many 'pieces of mind,' you're not going to have any left!* Instead of becoming offended at someone and taking matters into our own hands, we could simply choose to let a matter drop.

Kindness can also mean being humble enough to serve someone that you know has said something bad about you. Your flesh may want to put up a fight and get even, but the love of God that's been shed abroad in your heart by the Holy Ghost is gentle and mild in such cases.

Love Is Not Envious or Jealous

Second Corinthians 13:4 also says, *". . . love never is envious nor boils over with jealousy . . . "* (Amplified). Some people become offended because of envy or jealousy when someone else has more than they do. It seems they are constantly trying to catch up or keep up with someone else's level of prosperity.

Do you want to know God's way to catch up and even get ahead in life? *Refuse offense.* Refuse to give place to envy or jealousy. Rejoice with someone who receives a blessing. For example, if you want a new house and someone else you know gets a new house, rejoice with that person. Send him a housewarming gift or a card of congratulations. Pray for his continued blessings. You will reap a rich harvest of blessing for the blessing you sow into someone else's life.

Love Is Not Boastful, Proud, or 'Puffed Up'

The last part of First Corinthians 13:4 says that love *". . . is not boastful or vainglorious, does not display itself haughtily"* (Amplified). In other words, a person who's walking in the God-kind of love will not boast or brag about what he has or does. And he will not exhibit a "holier-than-thou" attitude!

Every person who has accepted Christ as Savior and Lord is a born-again child of God. And we already read that God the Father is no respecter of persons (Acts 10:34). In other words, He loves all of His children just the same.

So if we've stood in faith for something and we've been mindful to love and obey God and to love others as He has loved us, that doesn't give us bragging rights! We don't have the right to stick our thumbs under our lapels, so to speak, and have an attitude that we're better than others.

Christians also display a proud, haughty attitude when they're critical of others who may have sinned or missed the mark in some way. For example, I've heard Christians say about a brother or sister in the Lord, "He wouldn't be in the mess he's in if he hadn't done that. *I* would never do what *he* did!"

But they really don't know *what* they'd do if they were facing the same set of circumstances. Even if they did face similar challenges and passed the test, so to speak, they shouldn't be arrogant about it.

I feel heartbroken when I hear believers say about someone who experienced a tragedy, "Well, if he'd had any faith, that wouldn't have happened" or, "Maybe he sinned, and that's why this is happening to him."

Friend, that is a proud, condescending attitude no child of God should have. We who have been saved from a sinner's hell should be keenly aware that we are nothing on our own. The Bible says that God loved us while we were sinners (see Rom. 5:8). Jesus came down to where we were—down to our level—to save us. Now we should be willing to reach down to someone who has fallen and extend an arm of help, strength, comfort, and hope.

Instead, some groups, especially in Word-of-faith or charismatic circles, think they're the "only game in town." It's one thing to have pride in your church or to be proud of your spiritual roots or heritage, but it's another thing altogether to be haughty or smug about it.

God has people all over the world who are doing great things for His Kingdom. He has a plan for each person's life. And each church has a plan and purpose, a God-ordained vision, to fulfill as well. We should be honored to serve alongside one another instead of being competitive and allowing ourselves to be motivated by petty jealousies or by feelings of superiority.

I don't have to see eye-to-eye with every Christian I fellowship with. In other words, I may not completely agree with another minister's doctrine, and he may not agree with mine. But that doesn't mean we can't enjoy rich fellowship with each other around the doctrine of Jesus' shed blood at Calvary for the remission of our sins.

I once heard an informal definition of fellowship as *two fellows in the same ship*. There are many people in charismatic circles who will fellowship with me around the subject of salvation through Christ alone. And they're with me on the baptism in the Holy Spirit with the evidence of speaking in other tongues. They're even with me on the subject of divine healing. But the minute I mention prosperity, those fellows jump out of the ship! Yet I personally never have a problem with people not agreeing with me on every scriptural point. We must remember that we are all equal members of Christ's Body, purchased by His shed blood.

Love Is Not Conceited

First Corinthians 13:5 says, *"It [love] is not conceited (arrogant and inflated with pride); it is not rude (unmannerly) and does not act unbecomingly . . . "* (Amplified). Love is not rude! People who are walking in love don't act unbecomingly. In other words, they have and exhibit manners.

A person is not well-mannered if he pushes his way to the front of a crowd so he doesn't have to wait in line. The

Bible says, *"Be kindly affectioned one to another with broth-erly love; in honour preferring one another"* (Rom. 12:10). You're not preferring others if you're pushing them as you force your way past them!

Ministers usually receive special seating at big meetings and conferences, and that's a good thing. From time to time, ministers need to get away from constantly giving out to others so they can just receive spiritually from other men and women of God. But it comes across as very arrogant when a minister expects special seating, parking, and so forth—and becomes upset and offended when he doesn't get it or when he doesn't get the seat or parking space he wants.

I'm sure some ministers would occasionally like to go into a service, take a seat in the back of the sanctuary or auditorium, and just worship God without being recog-nized. I would like to do that, too, at times! On the other hand, it seems as if some ministers just desire to be seen and recognized. I'm not questioning the motives of every minister who attends another minister's conference; I'm simply saying that these things do happen, and it isn't very becoming.

Love Does Not Insist on Its Own Way

First Corinthians 13:5 also says, *". . . Love (God's love in us) does not insist on its own rights or its own way, for it is not self-seeking . . . "* (Amplified). Problems occur in our personal lives and in our relationships when we fail to develop this facet of God's love.

Let's look at what James had to say about the dangers of selfishness and of being self-seeking.

JAMES 3:16 (NKJV)
16 For where envy and SELF-SEEKING exist, confusion and every evil thing are there.

JAMES 3:16 (NIV)
16 For where you have envy and SELFISH AMBITION, there you find disorder and every evil practice.

So many problems would be solved in the Body of Christ if each member began seeking God's interests instead of his or her own interests. But when Christians begin seeking to fulfill their own selfish ambitions and desires—seeking only what's best for them—the Bible says *every* evil practice is present!

That's pretty serious! We should eagerly strive to seek God's interests and the interests of others over our own interests. To the carnal or natural man, that doesn't make sense, because in his mind, to seek someone else's interests instead of his own could prove to be harmful to him. But Jesus laid that idea to rest when He talked about preferring and serving others in Matthew 19:30 (NKJV) and Mark 10:31 (NKJV): *". . . many who are first will be last, and the last first."*

Love Is Not Easily Offended

The next part of verse 5 says, *". . . it [God's love in us] is not touchy or fretful or resentful . . . "* (Amplified).

Do you know people who are so touchy that you have to carefully guard every word you say to them? It seems as if you have to "tiptoe" around people like this so that you don't awaken full-scale emotion! The least thing you say could make them upset and offended. Obviously, people like this will usually misconstrue what you say to mean you're somehow putting them down. And then you have some real pouting to deal with!

These kinds of people have not developed their love walk as they should. They have some more work to do in allowing the God-kind of love to shine past their emotions and manifest itself in and through their lives.

Love Overlooks an Offense!

We've been talking about love not giving or receiving offense. This phrase in the last part of verse 5 says, *"love takes no account of the evil done to it [it pays no attention to a suffered wrong]"* (Amplified). This is specifically talking about forgiving and not taking offense.

The person who's walking in love "takes no account" of evil that's committed against him. In other words, that person doesn't try to get even with the individual who wrongs him. He pays no attention to the suffered wrong. That means he doesn't allow the injustice to take up dwelling in his thought life. He refuses to give it the attention it's demanding in an attempt to try to throw him off track spiritually.

Just recently, someone approached me and asked me, "Have you heard what So-and-so said about you?" and he proceeded to repeat what the person had said.

I interrupted him, saying, "Well, God bless him. We love him," and I began to talk about something else!

The person looked at me sort of strange, because I'm sure he was expecting a different response! But I don't have time to get into strife with people and to become offended. I have too much at stake spiritually to allow myself to become entangled with that kind of nonsense.

So what do I do when the chance to become offended presents itself? I "take no account" and I "pay no attention"! Try it—you'll find that it will work wonders in your life too!

Love Doesn't Rejoice at Injustice

First Corinthians 13:6 says, *"It* [love] *does not rejoice at injustice and unrighteousness, but rejoices when right and truth prevail"* (Amplified).

One of the distinguishing characteristics of a person who has allowed offense to become rooted within them is the desire for revenge or for "getting even." Someone who's offended at a person that experiences some kind of tragedy or hardship will think, *Good! I'm glad—he had it coming to him!*

'Father, Forgive Them'

The greatest act of forgiveness—and the greatest example of refusing offense—was accomplished by Jesus Christ on the Cross of Calvary. The greatest evidence of

Jesus' attitude toward those who crucified him can be found in some of His last words on the Cross: *". . . Father, forgive them; for they know not what they do. . ."* (Luke 23:34).

Notice Jesus *didn't* say, "Father, kill them all! Pay them back for the wrong they're committing!" Instead, He showed mercy as He forgave His offenders and asked the Father not to hold their sins against them.

Have *you* ever asked God not to hold a person's sin against him after the person offended you in some way? I heard my dad say many times when he was wronged by others, "Father, forgive them. Bless them. I don't want to see them cursed; I want to see them blessed."

This is the attitude we must maintain if we are to avoid the trap of being offended. Yet when someone does something to hurt us, how often do we make comments such as, "Well, what goes around comes around. You reap what you sow. He'll get what's coming to him one day, just wait and see"? It's almost as if we're *hoping* he gets what's coming to him sooner and not later!

But the Bible plainly says that if we're operating in the God-kind of love, we will not rejoice at another's hardship— even if he did perhaps bring it on himself. Instead, the person who is walking in love will have compassion on that other person and even pray for him—and desire bless-ing, not cursing, to come to him. Why? Because someone who's operating in the love of God only rejoices when God's rightness and truth prevail.

Love Believes the Best

First Corinthians 13:7 says, *"Love bears up under anything and everything that comes, is ever ready to believe the best of every person, its hopes are fadeless under all circumstances, and it endures everything [without weaken-ing]"* (Amplified).

Some people who don't understand spiritual things view walking in this kind of love as a weakness. But God *is* love (1 John 4:8), and there is nothing weak about God Almighty! And when we walk in the light of His love, we have His strength at our disposal. When we walk in love, we possess supernatural strength to undergo tough situa-tions without buckling and to come through each test or trial victorious.

However, our love walk is weakened when we fail to abide in the love of God. For example, verse 7 says His love in us *"... is ever ready to believe the best of every person.... "*

So if we're ready to believe the *worst,* we're not abiding in God's love as we should be.

Did you know it is possible to see someone miss it and sin, yet still wholeheartedly believe in that person? How do I know that? Because we've *all* missed it on some point, or on some level! And God never stopped believing in us; He never gave up on us. Proverbs 24:16 says, *"for though a righteous man falls seven times, he rises again...."* The Lord is able to lift him up and make him to stand firm!

Even when someone has committed some wrong against me, I often remark, "I still believe in him. I believe he'll make it. God is working in him and with him. I believe a change is coming."

Divine love is ready to believe the best, not the worst!

One reason gossip is spread is that people like believing the worst about people rather than the best. For example, someone might hear something bad about another person and, without even bothering to check it out, will begin telling others. The person who first got wind of the gossip just believed what he heard hook, line, and sinker, and started spreading it around. Of course, after the gossip spread to the third or fourth person, the story was probably already altered to point of being completely fictitious!

I remember an old game many of us used to play as kids in which two lines were formed, and the person at the head of each line would whisper something into the ear of the second person in each line. The second person in turn whispered the phrase to the third person in line, and so on. The line that communicated the phrase to the person at the end of the line the fastest won the game.

Finally, the person at the end of the line shouted out the phrase he thought he'd heard. More often than not, what he yelled out wasn't even *close* to what the first person in line actually said!

We simply can't believe everything we hear—especially if what we hear is about someone else. And even if something is true, that doesn't give us the right to propagate it all over the church, school, or neighborhood! (We'll talk more about that later in the book.)

I encourage you to write or type these verses from First Corinthians 13:4–8 on an index card or small piece of paper that you can carry with you. You could even laminate the paper and keep it in your wallet where you keep your bank cards. Review these scriptures periodically, or if you feel tempted to be impatient, unkind, and so forth, you can take out these verses and read them to yourself quietly if you're in public, or out loud if you're by yourself.

God's Word is His power for whatever we need if we'll believe Him and apply ourselves to His Word. This also includes what His Word has to say about love.

Offended Because of Righteousness

People operating in the God-kind of love conduct themselves in such a way that they don't give offense or take offense. Don't misunderstand me. I'm not saying that just because a person is walking in love, no one will ever become offended at him or her. For example, did Jesus walk in love during His earthly ministry? Of course He did. Yet many were offended at Him.

Remember I said that sometimes people will become offended at you when you're doing something *right*. This happened to Jesus often. He wasn't giving an offense; He was simply doing what the Father told Him to do. And you are not better than Jesus your master. If people became offended at Him as He obeyed God, people will also become offended at you as you obey God.

MARK 6:2–3

2 And when the sabbath day was come, he began to teach in the synagogue: and many hearing him were astonished, saying, From whence hath this man these things?

and what wisdom is this which is given unto him, that even such mighty works are wrought by his hands?

3 Is not this the carpenter, the son of Mary, the brother of James, and Joses, and of Juda, and Simon? and are not his sisters here with us? AND THEY WERE OFFENDED AT HIM.

Allow me to paraphrase in modern-day language what these people were perhaps saying about Jesus: "Hey, we know this guy! We know his family and his background. None of his family is a preacher; they're all carpenters. His dad just helped So-and-so remodel his kitchen! Jesus can't just get up and speak the Word of God like he owns the place! Who does he think he is, anyway?"

Of course, I'm speculating as to the exact words spoken against Jesus. But even today people are really no different from people back then. And they say some of the same things today when they're offended that people said in Jesus' day.

Here is an important point you need to remember. When people look at you in the natural, they can sometimes become offended when they see you fulfilling the will of God for your life. Some of our RHEMA Bible Training Center students can attest to that fact. Many have graduated from the school and have gone back to their home churches only to have certain people take the following attitude toward them: *I remember him from 'back when.' Who does he think he is trying to tell me anything? Does he think he's better than me now?*

I have experienced this kind of offense myself. Years ago after graduating from Bible college, I went back to visit my hometown in Texas. Some of my old friends said to me, "What! *A preacher?* Hagin, you're no preacher!"

Some of my old friends taunted me because they were under conviction. They weren't fulfilling the call of God on their own lives, so they persecuted me because I *was* fulfilling God's call. When they saw that I was doing what God had called me to do, instead of repenting for their disobedience, they became offended.

When people become offended at you for doing what's right, be very careful not to allow that situation to influence you to take offense at their offense! If *you* become offended because *they're* offended, you'll *both* find yourselves in a ditch!

Are You Offensive?

In teaching on the subject of offense, I often ask people, "Are you offensive toward others?" We spend so much time dealing with those who have been wounded by offense that we can overlook touching on "the other side of the coin."

In a previous chapter, we looked at the high cost of taking offense and harboring a grudge. But there also is a price to pay for being insensitive to others when we say or do something that is hurtful.

If we habitually offend people, not only are we grieving the Holy Spirit and the heart of God, we may also experience loss in the area of broken relationships. The following scripture gives us some insight into the high cost of being offensive to others.

PROVERBS 18:19

19 A brother offended is harder to be won than a strong city: and their contentions are like the bars of a castle.

PROVERBS 18:19 (NIV)

19 An offended brother is more unyielding than a fortified city, and disputes are like the barred gates of a citadel.

PROVERBS 18:19 (NLT)

19 It's harder to make amends with an offended friend than to capture a fortified city. Arguments separate friends like a gate locked with iron bars.

We have determined that holding on to offense can destroy you, but being offensive to others is equally wrong. People can sometimes be insensitive to others when they should be showing sympathy and compassion.

Sometimes people do offend others unintentionally, and I'm not talking about that. The Bible says, *"We all stumble in many ways. If anyone is never at fault in what he says, he is a perfect man, able to keep his whole body in check"* (James 3:2 NIV). However, I'm referring to believers who knowingly and callously offend with their words or actions and then leave the person they wounded to "deal with it." I'm talking about people who don't even try to make amends. Jesus makes a stern reference to those who cause the "little ones" to stumble into sin through offense (Matt. 18:6; Mark 9:42; Luke 17:2).

The main focus of this book is to warn believers of the dangers of holding on to offenses. My goal is to help Christians avoid the trap of becoming offended, or to help them free themselves from this potentially deadly snare if they've already allowed offenses to take root within. But the love of God that's in us never receives *or gives* an offense. Many a godly relationship has been needlessly and carelessly destroyed through offense.

Love Does Not Humiliate Others

We talked about the problems that occur when people spread gossip, and we said that often a story that gets passed from person to person usually ends up becoming only a half-truth or even a complete falsehood.

But what if you knew something about someone and you were absolutely certain it was completely true? Would it be okay to talk about it then?

Often when a person is offended at someone, the "gloves come off," so to speak, and the person who's been offended will yield to the temptation to talk badly about that person behind his or her back. The person who's harboring an offense might spread malicious gossip about the person, whereas before the offense occurred, the person who got hurt would never have dreamed of doing such a thing. This person has become distracted from obeying Jesus' new commandment of love.

JOHN 13:34

34 A new commandment I give unto you, That ye love one another; as I have loved you, that ye also love one another.

Another great attribute of God's love is, it covers sin. I didn't say it *condoned* sin; I said it doesn't make an open display of other people's faults, failures, and shortcomings.

> 1 PETER 4:8 (NKJV)
>
> 8 And above all things have fervent love for one another, for "love will cover a multitude of sins."

> 1 PETER 4:8 (NIV)
>
> 8 Above all, love each other deeply, because love covers over a multitude of sins.

Weymouth's translation says, "*. . . for love throws a veil over a multitude of faults.*"

So you see, a person who's yielding to and walking in the God-kind of love doesn't spread news about another person's personal problems. In other words, *love will stop offense in its tracks, because love will refuse to pass the offense on to others.*

Love Is Our 'Rulebook'

It's so important to keep the Word of God before your eyes and in your heart, because what you feed on continually is what you're eventually going to act on. But if you're continually dwelling on what someone has done to you, you're going to act on it, and you're going to be taking a step out of love *into* sin.

2 CORINTHIANS 5:14 (NKJV)

14 For the love of Christ compels us. . . .

The *Contemporary English Version* says, *"We are ruled by Christ's love for us. . . ."*

The *English Standard Version* says, *"For the love of Christ controls us. . . ."*

Weymouth's translation says, *"For the love of Christ overmasters us. . . ."*

In other words, love is to be our "rulebook." The God-kind of love must guide our affairs and determine the moves we make in the game of life.

No Love, No Light

I know of people who are constantly complaining about one thing or the other going wrong in their lives. They continually compare themselves to others and find themselves coming up short. For example, they'll say, "It seems everyone around me is getting blessed, but I'm not getting anything." The more they complain, the worse things seem, and their load just seems to increase. These people have become steeped in offense until it has become a way of life for them.

Once a person resorts to constant complaining, he ceases to be thankful or grateful in his heart for the things that are going right in his life. The Bible talks about the consequences of being unthankful—a heart that is darkened (see Rom. 1:21). A person who is thankful for the good in his life has chosen to rise above the opportunity to complain and take hold of offense. This person can then operate with God's light in his life.

Let Go of the Weight!

Do you carry around baggage from the past? Have you taken account of a suffered wrong when you should have forgiven the one who wronged you? Have you paid so much attention to the offense committed that it has consumed your life, weighed you down, and paralyzed you from moving forward toward your own happiness and dreams?

You cannot move forward with God if you're burdened down with offense. I have heard people testify that when they finally let go of the offense that had weighed them down, they began to feel better spiritually, mentally, emotionally, and physically. Life just seemed to look rosier. And eventually, even their circumstances began to turn around for the better. Why? Because they let go of the weight that had bound them. They stepped into the light and away from the shadows that had darkened their paths. So choose to let go of offenses that can weigh you down and choose to step into the freedom of God's light.

Chapter 8

Love Can Grow

To grow a garden successfully, you can't plant starters or seeds and then just leave them there unattended and expect them to grow. No, you have to water and fertilize a garden properly if you want the best harvest. You have to weed your garden and protect the plants from insects and pests that could ruin the work you've done.

In the same way, spiritual things, such as love, must be cultivated in order to grow. In other words, you can't just plant the Word of God in your heart and then neglect it. No, you have to water the seed of the Word that's been planted in your heart by continuing in the Word—reading, studying, and meditating on it. And you have to guard the "soil" of your heart against the enemies that would try to steal your harvest.

I THESSALONIANS 3:12

12 And the Lord make you to INCREASE and ABOUND in love one toward another, and toward all men, even as we do toward you.

As we yield ourselves to Him, the Lord will cause us to increase and abound—*to grow*—in love. Love must be cultivated in our lives, much like a garden is cultivated.

When you apply yourself to cultivating love in your life, your love will *grow.*

My dad's oldest brother, my Uncle Dub Hagin, whom I have previously mentioned, knew the reality of harboring offense and becoming embittered at a very young age. Uncle Dub, like my dad, had a very rough childhood. Since Dub was the oldest child, he bore the brunt of the hardships the children faced.

Uncle Dub grew up with a chip on his shoulder and left home as a very young man to make his way in life. Uncle Dub was tough—if anyone tried to cross him, he knew how to take care of them, and he wouldn't hesitate to do it! He didn't have a great deal of love for people, and this showed in his stride, his demeanor, and the way he talked and carried out his business.

Uncle Dub had a reputation for being violent at times. If someone got in his way, he would physically knock them down! And he was so strong that not too many people would ever make an issue of anything where he was concerned. They just steered clear of him.

After Uncle Dub finally turned his life over to God and began serving Him wholeheartedly, he really had to make an effort to walk in love. He told me once that he often meditated on First Corinthians 13:4–8 and First, Second, and Third John. He said, "I find that I have to do that regularly if I'm going to be able to walk in love."

Uncle Dub made the effort to correct a problem, and over time, he changed. In fact, he made great strides spiritually, because there's power in the Word of God! But notice that he went to the Word for help. He didn't make the excuse, as so many people do: "Well, this is just the way I am, and I'll always be this way. You're just going to have to live with it and deal with it."

Uncle Dub was not terribly unique in that there are many people who have a problem walking in love because of their difficult past. Naturally speaking, they have a right to be offended because of the awful wrongs committed against them. But just because they have a right to be offended doesn't mean that their offense will profit them.

On the contrary, that offense will eventually destroy them if they don't make a change.

But they can change it if they want to! Love is the way. They can grow in the love of God and become the kind of person they were meant to be—just as a plant grows and eventually produces the beautiful harvest it was intended to yield.

Love Must Grow in Good 'Soil'

To grow in love requires effort. We don't accidentally grow in spiritual things any more than we would accidentally grow a prize-winning crop of flowers, fruit, or vegetables.

To grow in love, just as in growing a garden, we must make sure that the soil of our heart is soft, not hard. We must be certain that our heart is free of "weeds" that could choke the life of our harvest.

I don't know a lot about farming, but I remember watching my grandpa and grandma as a very young boy as they hoed the rows of their cotton patch. After it rained, the hot Texas sun would bake that old "black land" soil, and a crust would form on the top of the ground. Grandma and Grandpa would use those hoes to loosen the dirt so that when they watered the crop or when it rained again, the ground would soak up the moisture and nourishment. Without loosening the soil, the water would have run off the surface, unable to penetrate the top layer of dirt.

To grow in love, we must continually cultivate love and carefully guard our hearts so that they do not become hard and incapable of bearing fruit. This cultivation will take diligent effort on our part. But we are not without help! God has given ample tools to ensure that love grows and increases in our hearts and lives.

We Must *Think* With Love

To grow in love, you must first *think* with love.

PHILIPPIANS 4:8

8 Finally, brethren, whatsoever things are true, whatso-ever things are honest, whatsoever things are just, whatsoever things are pure, whatsoever things are lovely, whatsoever things are of good report; if there be any virtue, and if there be any praise, THINK ON THESE THINGS.

Many Christians are very lax when it comes to their thought-life and thinking the right thoughts. They allow their minds to wander and to meditate and dwell on the wrong things. They do it mostly out of habit. They've been dwelling on "what someone did to me" for so long that it's easier to continue thinking that way than to force their mind to think in a different, new, and better direction—to the Word of God!

For example, it's easier to blame someone else for their present situation than it is to do something about extracting themselves from the situation.

I often tell people, "It may be someone else's fault that you're in the position you're in. But it's *your* fault if you stay there!"

No one has been so deeply hurt in life that he can't extract himself from the prison of offense that has held him captive. He can be set free, but it all begins with his thought-life. He must first change the way he thinks.

To grow in love and rise above offense, you must replace your negative thoughts with positive thoughts. I'm not saying that it will be easy. You may even have to quote Scripture every time a negative thought comes to you to distract you from the decision you've made to forgive. You may have to burn the midnight oil, so to speak, reading and meditating on portions of Scripture that cover whatever area of life you need help in, just as my Uncle Dub did.

The devil is the god of this world system (2 Cor. 4:4), and our natural minds are in constant contact with the world. That's why the Apostle Paul wrote in Romans 12:2, *"And be not conformed to this world: but be ye transformed by the renewing of your mind, that ye may prove what is that good, and acceptable, and perfect, will of God."* We simply can't allow ourselves to be conformed to what we constantly hear and see on television, in movies, and other media.

If you read the newspaper or watch a news broadcast, writers, anchors, and commentators will fill your mind with negativism. Even some ministers preach depressing messages on "the whole world going to hell in a handbasket."

I'm not saying we should stick our heads in the sand and ignore a lost and dying world. We should be about our Father's business of reaping the fields that are white with harvest (see John 4:35). But on the other hand, we don't need to see the reaping of the harvest as a hopeless endeavor.

For example, the way some ministers and news people talk, our young people have gone to the dogs! There could be 150 teenagers living right before God, but all we seem to hear about are a few that are being disruptive and problematic.

Also, have you ever noticed that the news media have a tendency to dig up dirt on people and then report it to the masses—and they do it without apology or regret? I mean, a person could be a public servant in his 30s or 40s, and members of the press will find something the person did wrong when he was a teenager or when he was in college, and they will broadcast his mistake for the world to see. What that person did may have no relevance on his life now. Yet he must endure public humiliation because he's in the public eye, and because the majority of our media is under the world's system.

Similarly, an individual's constant focus on what someone else did to hurt him comes from the "god of this world," Satan. Harboring offense goes completely against the Word of God. That's why we're going to have to choose which side we're on—we must choose what we're going to think and dwell on. If we choose rightly, we can walk free of the pain of the past. But if we choose to dwell on the evil that occurred, that evil will become a stronghold in our lives.

There is a law of attraction that says what you consistently think about and believe, you will attract and draw to yourself. From a biblical perspective, that's true. What you think long enough, you will eventually believe. What you believe long enough, you will eventually act on or do.

God told the Israelites, *"I call heaven and earth to record this day against you, that I have set before you life and death, blessing and cursing: therefore CHOOSE LIFE, that both thou and thy seed may live"* (Deut. 30:19). In other words, we have a choice as to what we will think about, focus on, and do.

We have more to say about our success or failure in life than we've realized! We can think on what God has to say in His Word, and watch our lives begin to line up with "life more abundantly" (John 10:10). Or we can think on the enemy's thoughts, and discover that destruction is holding a very prominent place in our lives.

If we will not change our thought processes to line up with God's Word, we will not grow in love.

We Must *Look* With Love

In Luke 19:41 we read that as Jesus neared the city of Jerusalem, He wept over it. As He beheld the city, He realized their plight and their dimness of sight that caused them to miss the day of their visitation by God.

Christ had compassion even on those who rejected Him, hindering His ability to help them. He looked on people bound by sin. He looked on those who were considered the "less fortunate" in society. He looked on the multitudes with their many needs. And He was moved with compassion toward all of them!

Matthew 9:36 says, *"But when he SAW the multitudes, he was moved with compassion on them, because they fainted, and were scattered abroad, as sheep having no shepherd."* Jesus was moved with compassion because He was looking with love.

Jesus looked past the helpless, hopeless, and sick multitudes into the hearts of individuals. He was moved with compassion to minister to their needs.

Likewise, when we look around us, we need to see more than a neighbor, a housewife, a doctor, a policeman, a teacher, or a student—we need to see individual people with individual needs that God can meet through a heart that is His.

Too often we look at others, especially those who are unkind, with criticism and skepticism instead of with love and compassion. We need to look with love past the faults, failures, and shortcomings of others.

A Christian could miss it and sin, repent before God according to First John 1:9, and be forgiven, cleansed, and restored by God. Yet among his fellow church members, he often finds anything but forgiveness and restoration. Instead, he may face coldness, hardness, criticism, and rejection. Those people who reject the brother or sister who falls aren't looking at that person with love—they haven't cultivated love as they should.

GALATIANS 6:1

1 Brethren, if a man be overtaken in a fault, ye which are spiritual, restore such an one in the spirit of meekness; considering thyself, lest thou also be tempted.

When we hear of someone who has made a mistake and has been overtaken in a sin, our first thoughts should be, *If I were in his position, how would I want to be treated? Would I want to be criticized and talked about, or would I want to be shown mercy and forgiveness?*

We Must *Listen* With Love

When people are crying out for help around us, often we are so busy and taken up with the cares of life, and even with the necessary tasks of life, that we don't really hear their cries and give them the help they need. Instead of offering up a quick prayer, "Lord, bless them," we need to develop a tender heart and a hearing ear toward those who are hurting.

Often when we do take the time to try to help someone in need, we want to do all the talking. We listen just a little bit and think we have the answer he needs all wrapped up in a nice, neat little package. Instead of bandaging the wound, we're just talking and not really helping at all.

If you were to skin your right knee, you wouldn't clean and bandage your left knee, would you? No, you would wash and bandage the area that was hurt. Similarly, if we want to grow in love, we must learn to listen with love so that we can be effective in ministering God's love and healing mercy where it is needed.

I will never forget the day years ago when Lynette and I sat across the table from a group of six doctors who told us that our son, Craig, had a tumor on his brain. We know what it's like to have the rug pulled from under us, so to speak, and to feel darkness and despair closing in around us. At that moment in time, we didn't need anyone shouting scriptures at us, letting us know what great faith he had. We had a deep-down sense that God was with us and that He would see us through. But what we needed right then was people who would put their arms around us and tell us they loved us and were standing with us. We needed people just to be with us and to listen in love.

We Must *Speak* With Love

Growing up, most of us have probably heard our parents say at one time or another, "If you can't think of something good to say about someone, don't say anything at all." That's good advice! We should all be mindful of the words we speak, especially words we speak about others.

There was a certain man in my dad's hometown many years ago who was mean and ruthless. He had a violent temper, and some said he wasn't right mentally—that he'd lost his mind during the time of his military service in World War I. Many were afraid of this man; no one liked him.

When this man died, many in the town attended his funeral. People would walk past his casket rehearsing to one another their bad experiences and not-so-fond memories in connection with this man.

As my dad used to tell the story, there was another man in that town who was a model believer in that he never spoke a bad word against anyone, *ever*. This believer attended the funeral too. And as he approached the casket, there was a sudden silence in the room as everyone seemed to stop what they were doing to hear what this believer would say about the man that had "terrorized" this small town.

The believer stood at the casket for a moment, silent. Then he leaned over as if to study the man inside or to get a closer look. Finally, he said, "Well, he did have nice teeth, didn't he?"

Vehicles of Power to Hurt or to Heal

Words are containers. They are filled either with faith, hope, love, and mercy, or they're filled with doubt, despair, fear, and hatred.

The words you speak can either cause someone to rise up to his full potential so that he can go out and win in life—or your words can cause him to fail. Your words can lift someone up who has fallen, or they can cause him to sink further into hopelessness and despair.

We need to refuse to use our mouths to speak condemnation to a brother or sister. Instead, our lips should be filled with love and compassion. With our words, we should usher brothers and sisters back into the family, rather than expelling them.

Growing in Love—Worth the Effort

Maturing in love and rising above offense isn't always going to be easy to do. But it is the *right* thing to do! My dad used to constantly tell me, "Son, if something's worth having, it's worth working for."

The things of God won't just "fall" on us without our making any effort to desire them and to position ourselves to receive them. Just as it takes a plant time to grow and bear fruit, we must grow in love.

Chapter 9

How to Resolve Conflicts

It's impossible to be a functioning member of society on this planet without experiencing conflict with another person at one time or another. You will encounter conflict in life, but you can handle each conflict skillfully, with the wisdom of God, and continue to walk in the love of God. Your ability to resolve conflict will go a long way in healing offenses and, more importantly, preventing them from occurring.

Conflict and Compromise

Conflicts arise in families from time to time. When Craig and Denise were younger and lived at home, one example of a light conflict in our family was in agreeing on where to eat!

If we were going to eat fast food, Craig liked Burger King, Denise liked McDonald's, I liked Whataburger, and Lynette didn't mind where we ate. Sometimes we would compromise and use the drive-through window at Burger King to get Craig's meal—then we'd go down the street a couple of miles to pick up Denise's meal at McDonald's. Last, we'd go to Whataburger. The kids would bring their meals into the Whataburger restaurant, and Lynette and I would order what we wanted to eat.

In those cases, compromise settled a conflict before there really ever *was* one! However, there were times when we needed to pick just one restaurant, and it was a challenge to have a good attitude when the family ate at a restaurant where one person didn't really want to go. One person may have said, "Well, okay," as the decision was made, but the person's attitude, including mine at times, might not always have been the best!

Conflicts can arise over anything—from disagreements over responsibilities between employees, roommates, and spouses, to issues involving doctrine, relationships, money, restaurant choices, and much more.

Do you know how to handle conflict? When conflict arises in your life, do your tactics lead to heated debate, strife, and more conflict? Do you simply refuse to deal with conflict by "going into hiding" and pretending it doesn't exist?

We need to learn how to handle conflicts when they arise, because conflicts that aren't dealt with will become opportunities for strife, confusion, and, inevitably, *offense.*

In this chapter, we will explore ways to resolve conflicts and keep ourselves in the love of God. And that will enable us to avoid the trap of being offended.

Number One: Open Your Heart

In Second Corinthians 7:2, Paul addressed a group of people about a conflict, or a potential for conflict, that existed between them.

2 CORINTHIANS 7:2 (NIV)
2 Make room for us in your hearts. We have wronged no one, we have corrupted no one, we have exploited no one.

In this verse, Paul is talking about *openness*—about being open with one another. To give you some brief background, the Church at Corinth, which Paul had founded, was upset because of the first letter he had written to them. In this first letter, he rebuked the church, and the people were upset because of Paul's reprimand. Perhaps they were angry that they even had to be corrected to begin with. Whatever the case, there was a stir among the church because of this letter.

2 CORINTHIANS 7:8 (NIV)

8 Even if I caused you sorrow by my letter, I do not regret it. Though I did regret it—I see that my letter hurt you, but only for a little while.

I'm sure Paul didn't enjoy having to bring such stern correction to the Corinthian church. He regretted that it needed to be done in the first place or that the recipients were stung and "made sorrowful" by his message (2 Cor. 7:8–9). But Paul didn't regret actually writing the letter reprimanding the church, because it needed to be written. He had to bring correction to them in the hope they would receive it and be brought to repentance. And the Bible says that they did indeed repent.

In the first part of chapter 7, Paul said, "Make room for us in your hearts. Although I wrote you that letter, open yourself to receive us. We have not wronged you." Paul was dealing with conflict or potential conflict in a relationship—in his own relationship with the Church at Corinth.

Before a conflict can be resolved, the parties involved must be willing to open their hearts and receive one another. Oftentimes, the reason conflict is not resolved is that one or more parties become close-minded. People will say things such as, "I don't like what So-and-so did, and I'm never going to speak to him again!" Those people aren't making room in their hearts for anyone—they're only making room for more conflict, offense, and trouble!

Sometimes you may have to be the first to say, "Hey, look, there's a problem. What can we do to resolve it?" You must do what you can to encourage openness, because without it, communication cannot continue.

In Second Corinthians chapter 6, Paul says something very interesting to the Corinthian believers along this line.

2 CORINTHIANS 6:11–13 (NIV)

11 We have spoken freely to you, Corinthians, and opened wide our hearts to you.

12 We are not withholding our affection from you, but you are withholding yours from us.

13 As a fair exchange—I speak as to my children—open wide your hearts also.

Have you ever tried to resolve a conflict with someone by saying, "Be truthful and tell me what you think"? Then if they told you what they thought, did you receive what he or she had to say, or did you escalate the conflict into a full-fledged war? If resolving conflict is really the goal, part of the resolution should include openness, both when you're speaking to someone *and* when you're listening to someone else speak! A "fair exchange" must be a part of the process.

If you're a parent of a teenager, you're aware that sometimes you may have to sit down and open your heart to your son or daughter and just be very open. You may have to talk to him or her about the rules of the house, because certain privileges have been misused or abused. If you're attempting to avoid more strife and conflict, the last thing you want is not to be received openly, because more conflict can occur!

Paul spoke very freely to the Corinthians when he said, *"We are not withholding our affection from you, but you are withholding yours from us"* (2 Cor. 6:12 NIV). In order to resolve the conflict and restore harmony to the relationship, the Corinthian church had to open their hearts to Paul and reciprocate the affection he showed in embracing this church in his heart. Paul said, *"As a fair exchange—I speak as to my children—open wide your hearts also"* (v. 13, NIV).

Number Two: Deal Squarely With the Issues

Paul dealt well with conflict in that he faced the issues instead of running from them. And in your own life, you cannot resolve conflict scripturally unless you are willing to face the issues and not dodge them.

Why do people hold on to offense when it would bless and benefit them so much more to deal with the conflict if it's possible, avoid the offense, and completely let it go? One reason is, they are yielding to the flesh, which always motivates a person to insist on his own rights and his own way. Consequently, they hold on tightly to such thoughts as, *I was mistreated! I have a right to feel this way after all I've suffered!*

Yielding to the flesh will also motivate a person to justify his or her behavior rather than repent. You show me someone who will never admit it when he's wrong, and I'll show you someone who's walking after the flesh, not after the Spirit!

How many times have you heard people say they wanted to resolve an issue, but they were unwilling to face the real issues, especially if any of those issues warranted their admitting fault or making some kind of change in their life?

If you're involved in a conflict, and you know you had a part to play, be accountable for your role in creating the disharmony. Face the issue squarely. It is still in good taste to say, "I'm sorry" when we miss it!

In the case of Paul and the Corinthian church, Paul put the issue squarely before them by saying, *"We have wronged no one."* In other words, Paul could have just as easily said to them, "You really don't have a leg to stand on feeling this way toward me and acting the way you're acting." Paul wasn't wrong to reprimand that church in his first letter. In fact, he was mandated by God to exhort and admonish them to continue in the same Gospel upon which the church was founded.

Notice that Paul didn't come across as hostile or agitated. Have you ever noticed that people who don't deal squarely with issues can be mean, cantankerous, and difficult to get along with? *Peaceful* and *tranquil* are not usually words you would choose to describe a person who does not handle conflict well! How much better to be open—to face issues directly in the right spirit—and resolve a conflict, rather than allow that conflict to fan into a raging fire of hatred and strife!

I have actually heard Christians say, "There's a problem, all right. But I'm going to deal with it by faith. I'm just going to believe God."

If we have faith that God is going to help us resolve conflict, then why not add some "works" to our faith? (See James 2:17–26.) Otherwise, we can pray till we're "blue in the face," and nothing will happen if we won't act on the truth we know.

It's good to pray about everything and to ask for God's help in resolving a conflict. But along with our believing, we need to be *doing* something. And Paul outlined some very good counsel in Second Corinthians chapter 7. In verse 2, he encouraged the Corinthians to *"make room for us in your hearts"* (NIV). He was urging them to be open to him and what he had to say. And in verse 9 he told them, *"Even if I caused you sorrow by my letter, I do not regret it"* (NIV), because the issue had to be addressed. He had to write to them and be direct with them for their own good.

"But I just believe God is going to handle it," someone may say. No, He won't work on your behalf until you cooperate with Him in the process. That means that when you do your part, He will certainly do His part!

If you choose to deal scripturally with conflict by meeting the issue head-on, there is no guarantee that the other person or group will participate equally and with the same amount of enthusiasm. But if they don't, you should not feel badly that the relationship wasn't restored. You can only decide for *yourself* how you will act in such a situation. And if you choose to handle conflict biblically, you can rest in the knowledge that you did the right thing.

Of course, this attitude doesn't work in conflicts between husband and wife. Unless the woman is being abused physically, a husband and wife should *never* give up trying to resolve conflict, make peace, and restore harmony. God's highest and best is that they dwell together in complete unity, glorifying Him and making tremendous power available as they pray together in agreement that His will and blessings be manifested in their lives (Matt. 18:19).

Number Three: Do Not Condemn

In Second Corinthians chapter 7, after Paul said, *"Make room for us in your hearts,"* he added, *"I do not say this to condemn you; I have said before that you have such a place in our hearts that we would live or die with you"* (vv. 2–3 NIV). A person who sincerely desires to resolve a conflict will never condemn the other person or persons, but will approach the situation with kindness and gentleness.

Unfortunately, some people who "come to the table" to resolve a matter want to leave that meeting saying, "I won." But if a conflict between two parties is resolved properly, both of them should be able to say, *"We* won," because a problem was solved and a relationship was salvaged. God's love was able to prevail—and that should spell victory in *anyone's* book!

When secular groups such as employers and unions resolve conflict and reach a compromise, both sides usually win, and the relationship between the two parties remains peaceable and workable.

Likewise, most people don't mind putting forth the effort to resolve a conflict if they go away from the meeting feeling as if they accomplished something and weren't just "trampled on." This is especially true of husbands and wives. Spouses should always walk away from a conflict with their unity completely restored instead of ending with unresolved issues and in a "stand-off" state.

When Paul said, *"You have such a place in my heart that I am willing to live or die with you,"* he was affirming his love for them and showing them he was willing to "go the extra mile." In other words, Paul was saying, "I'm willing to do whatever it takes to settle this thing."

In a letter Paul wrote to the Church at Thessalonica, he said something else that indicated his close relationship with the churches that he helped start.

1 THESSALONIANS 2:11–12 (NIV)

11 For you know that we dealt with each of you as a father deals with his own children,

12 encouraging, comforting and urging you to live lives worthy of God, who calls you into his kingdom and glory.

In this passage, Paul is "encouraging, comforting, and urging" the people to live as Christians, worthy of their calling. Paul wasn't lecturing or criticizing them—he was simply reminding them of who they were.

Whether a conflict exists between employers and employees, husbands and wives, parents and children, or among friends or co-workers, people have feelings—no matter who they are and regardless of their age or status in life. No one involved in a conflict should ever criticize or condemn another person so that the person feels worthless and hopeless. And if we each took the attitude, as Paul did, *"You have such a place in my heart,"* we never will!

Number Four: Make an Appeal for Unity

When we're faced with conflicts in life, we simply cannot afford to ignore them. As I said, we need to learn how to handle conflicts *when they arise,* because conflicts that are ignored will become opportunities for strife, offense, and confusion.

What would an orchestra sound like if the horn section were in conflict with the string and percussion sections? When the conductor picked up his baton and signaled the trombone players, the musicians would protest, saying, "No, we're going to play in *this* key instead." And the string musicians would say, "Oh, yeah, well we're going to play in *this* key!" Then the percussionists would throw off their headphones and say, "We're just going to do our own thing!" By the time they played a few measures, the audience would either walk out or scream, "Stop that noise!"

However, that same group of musicians could decide to follow the conductor's lead and play in harmony with one another, and the music would be beautiful.

What makes the difference? When the orchestra was in disharmony, they were all playing music, weren't they? And they may have each been played beautifully. But until they played in harmony—each in his or her respective notes and keys—there could be no real music.

Isn't that the way it is in life? For example, in an office all of the co-workers could be on the same page, so to speak, concerning a task or assignment, yet they could be operating in disharmony. For the most effective results, they need to work together to get the job done properly.

Number Five: Value the People Involved

In Second Corinthians 7:4, let's look at something else Paul said to indicate his sincerity toward the Corinthian believers and the value he placed on them as well as on his relationship with them.

2 CORINTHIANS 7:2–4 (NIV)

2 Make room for us in your hearts. We have wronged no one, we have corrupted no one, we have exploited no one.

3 I do not say this to condemn you; I have said before that you have such a place in our hearts that we would live or die with you.

4 I have great confidence in you; I take great pride in you. I am greatly encouraged; in all our troubles my joy knows no bounds.

Paul told the Corinthian believers, "I have great confidence in you; I take great pride in you. . . ." In order for conflicts to be resolved, the people involved must feel like they are loved and worthwhile. Paul was simply saying, "I believe in you."

This is exactly the way we need to deal with our children. Parents who communicate their faith and confidence in their children at an early age will likely have less conflict to deal with down the road. And when conflict does occur, both parties will be willing to resolve it, not just the parents.

Many times, teenagers are unwilling to try to work through difficulty in their relationship with their parents because those young people may feel worthless and hopeless. They don't want to listen to a parent just pointing out their mistakes. They need to know that their parent believes they can succeed in life no matter how badly they've failed in the past.

Paul was diligent to show his undying belief in the people of God that he had fathered in the faith.

2 CORINTHIANS 8:22, 24 (NIV)

22 In addition, we are sending with them our brother who has often proved to us in many ways that he is zealous, and now even more so because of his great confidence in you. . . .

24 Therefore show these men the proof of your love and the reason for our pride in you, so that the churches can see it.

Verse 24 in *The Amplified Bible* reads, *"Show to these men, therefore, in the sight of the churches, the reality and plain truth of your love (your affection, goodwill, and benevolence) and what [good reasons] I had for boasting about and being proud of you."*

Now look at Second Corinthians 9:2 (NIV): *"For I know your eagerness to help, and I have been boasting about it to the Macedonians, telling them that since last year you in Achaia were ready to give; and your enthusiasm has stirred most of them to action."* Because of Paul's confidence in the Corinthian church, he bragged about them to other churches he visited to help motivate other believers and stir them to action.

To settle a conflict, you must express confidence in the other party. If someone offended you, you need to say, "No matter what has happened, I still have confidence in you; I still believe in you." Building another person's feelings of self-worth makes him more eager to resolve a conflict and solidify the relationship.

Resolution and Healing

The last part of Second Corinthians 7:4 in the NIV says, "*. . . in all our troubles my joy knows no bounds.*" Paul's troubles were the afflictions he faced as he ministered the Gospel, often meeting with fierce opposition. Titus related Paul's troubles to the Corinthian church, and they showed great concern for Paul.

2 CORINTHIANS 7:7 (NIV)

7 and not only by his coming but also by the comfort you had given him. He told us about your longing for me, your deep sorrow, your ardent concern for me, so that my joy was greater than ever.

Paul was overjoyed that their conflict had been resolved and that the church had expressed devoted concern about his welfare. This was part of the healing process. A conflict was dealt with and resolved, and, afterward, healing between the two parties occurred.

Conflict resolution doesn't always happen overnight, especially if there has been conflict in relationship for years that has been silenced, either through ignorance or willfulness.

If you've not spoken to a loved one in years, I encourage you to resolve today to settle that issue between you. Even if the other person was the offender and perpetrator of the conflict, you can still take the first step!

Begin by forgiving the other person if you haven't already done so. Then try to establish some kind of openness. Perhaps you can open your heart to that person by writing a letter or sending an e-mail. You could say something such as, "Let's put this issue behind us."

Many times, all it takes is one small gesture on the part of one person to begin the process of resolving conflict and reestablishing valuable relationships. Even though the other person may not respond to the move you make to reconnect with him or her, *do it anyway.*

God knew that we would experience conflicts in life. If the Apostle Paul and the early church fathers faced conflict among themselves, we know we are not exempt from experiencing similar issues today. The key is to be willing and ready to resolve conflict as it comes. We can do that by being open, direct, gentle, and non-critical; by desiring restoration and unity; and by valuing all the people in our lives as precious and as those for whom Christ died.

Jesus said that the believer's joy is made full when he or she receives from God according to His Word (John 16:23–24). Jesus also said that in our receiving, God is glorified (John 15:7–8). Our walk with God and the testimony we share with the world around us, whether in word or deed, are crucial to our pleasing the Father and to our participating in the great harvest of souls.

So let's be diligent to put away those things that would hinder our fellowship with God and obscure our view of the One Who saved us. Let us remember that offense is an insidious enemy of the Church that has hindered us for too long. May we continue to strive for unity and endeavor to lift Jesus high, keep His commands, and walk as free men and women because of His great example and sacrifice. Let us avoid the trap of being offended by always walking in love toward others and by choosing to forgive.

Why should you consider attending

RHEMA
Bible Training Center?

Here are a few good reasons:

- Training at one of the top Spirit-filled Bible schools anywhere
- Teaching based on steadfast faith in God's Word
- Growth in your spiritual walk coupled with practical training in effective ministry
- Specialization in the area of your choosing: Youth or Children's Ministry, Evangelism, Pastoral Care, Missions, or Supportive Ministry
- Optional intensive third-year programs—School of Worship, School of Pastoral Ministry, School of World Missions, and General Extended Studies
- Worldwide ministry opportunities—while you're in school
- An established network of churches and ministries around the world who depend on RHEMA to supply full-time staff and support ministers

Call today for information or application material.
1-888-28-FAITH (1-888-283-2484)
www.rbtc.org

RHEMA Bible Training Center admits students of any race, color, or ethnic origin.

Always on.

For the latest news and information on products,
media, podcasts, study resources, and
special offers, visit us online 24 hours a day.

Free Subscription!

Call now to receive a free subscription to *The Word of Faith* magazine from Kenneth Hagin Ministries. Receive encouragement and spiritual refreshment from . . .

- *Faith-building articles from Kenneth W. Hagin, Lynette Hagin, and others*

- *"Timeless Teaching" from the archives of Kenneth E. Hagin*

- *Feature articles on prayer and healing*

- *Testimonies of salvation, healing, and deliverance*

- *Children's activity page*

- *Updates on RHEMA Bible Training Center, RHEMA Bible Church, and other outreaches of Kenneth Hagin Ministries*

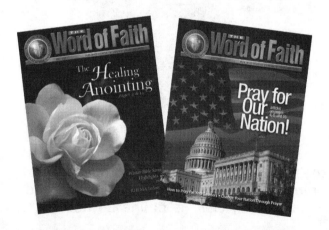

Subscribe today for your free *Word of Faith*!

1-888-28-FAITH (1-888-283-2484)

www.rhema.org/wof

OFFER CODE—BKORD:WF

RHEMA
Correspondence Bible School

The RHEMA Correspondence Bible School is a home Bible study course that can help you in your everyday life!

This course of study has been designed with you in mind, providing practical teaching on prayer, faith, healing, Spirit-led living, and much more to help you live a victorious Christian life!

Flexible
Enroll any time: choose your topic of study;
study at your own pace!

Affordable
Pay as you go—only $25 per lesson!
(Price subject to change without notice.)

Profitable

"The Lord has blessed me through a RHEMA Correspondence Bible School graduate. . . . He witnessed to me 15 years ago, and the Lord delivered me from drugs and alcohol. I was living on the streets and then in somebody's tool shed. Now I lead a victorious and blessed life! I now am a graduate of RHEMA Correspondence Bible School too! I own a beautiful home. I have a beautiful wife and two children who also love the Lord. The Lord allows me to preach whenever my pastor is out of town. I am on the board of directors at my church and at the Christian school. Thank you, and God bless you and your ministry!"

—D.J., Lusby, Maryland

"Thank you for continually offering RHEMA Correspondence Bible School. The eyes of my understanding have been enlightened greatly through the Word of God through having been enrolled in RCBS. My life has forever been changed."

—M.R., Princeton, N.C.